Don't be fooled by her name – Del  have had 30 years of experience in and publishing.

An enthusiastic writer and blogger, she now draws on her past lives to help new authors sell their books with her consultancy, Off The Shelf Book Promotions. Find out more at www.otsbp.com.

To the benefit of authors everywhere, she is also helping to raise a new generation of enthusiastic readers by working part-time at the national children's reading charity, Readathon (www.readathon.org).

Born and raised in Sidcup, Kent, she now lives in a small Gloucestershire village with her Scottish husband and their daughter. One day, she hopes to have read all the books on her "must read" list – and to catch up on her sleep.

Debbie's personal blog is at www.youngbyname.me.

25% of the author's royalties will be donated to the Juvenile Diabetes Research Foundation, working towards a cure for Type 1 Diabetes. Find out more at www.jdrf.org.uk.

Sell Your Books!
A book promotion handbook for the self-published or indie author
DEBBIE YOUNG

Foreword by Dr Alison Baverstock
Course Leader for MA Publishing at Kingston University

SilverWood

Published in paperback and e-book by SilverWood Originals 2012

SilverWood Originals is a small press imprint of SilverWood Books
30 Queen Charlotte Street, Bristol, BS1 4HJ
Find out more at
www.silverwoodbooks.co.uk/silverwood-originals

SilverWood Originals – traditional publishing at its best

ISBN 978-1-906236-34-2
Also available as an e-book
e-pub ISBN 978-1-78132-031-0

British Library Cataloguing in Publication Data
A CIP catalogue record for this book is available from the British Library

Set in Sabon and Univers by SilverWood Books
Printed on paper sourced responsibly

Contents

Foreword

by Dr Alison Baverstock

I admire the honesty of this book's title. "Selling" is a word many people avoid; it tends to get disguised in job titles, and certainly in the long preambles from those offering unrequested but "important customer information" by telephone.

As a process, selling is obviously vital – anyone with a product or service to sell needs to find customers willing to buy. If nothing is sold, there is no revenue to compensate for the costs incurred in production, distribution and marketing – and of course to feed into the development of further ideas. For publishers, gaining sales revenue is particularly crucial. One of the many problems for the industry is that nearly all the costs come early, but you have nothing to sell until the product is finished.

In the past, writers have often preferred to separate themselves from the process of selling, relying on their publishers to do the work for them. This is understandable. Just because you can write does not necessarily qualify you to talk up your work in public. But today even authors with loyal publishing houses can no longer delegate the selling process to investors and friends; they too must enter the fray. And if you are self-publishing, assuming responsibility for selling your work is one of the biggest surprises – it can take as much time and effort as the writing.

Why? Because the market is getting harder to reach; the sheer range of media through which you can hear about books worth reading means that no longer can you rely on a good review in a national newspaper to ensure that everyone is aware. Values are also changing. Today speed of access tends to be prized over concern about who compiled the material sought – and quality-driven authors need to assert the value of carefully developed content that has been presented with care. Authors need to be part of the debate about how writing is regarded and valued by society – and absolutely unashamed to make work they value available for others to enjoy.

Even unwilling participants can learn to understand their customers (publishers, agents, retailers and literary festival managers as well as readers), and their various requirements. They must somehow manage the tightrope of making work known without removing the need to read (or preferably own) the book. And they must balance the amount of time they spend selling with the investment of energy in actually producing work – readers sense pretty soon if a writer's point of main effort is promotion rather than the crafting of something worth reading.

This book will help. It provides motivating, practical and cheerful guidance on the process. It raises the spirits and promotes author confidence. It's an investment in your writing now – and your future development.

Ultimately, revenue apart, sales matter to the writer because they generally indicate how widely you are being read. If your work sells you remain discoverable – and a pathway to the real highlights of the writer's life opens up – perhaps seeing your work displayed in a bookshop or hearing from an individual reader that something you wrote has been valued by them. For anyone who seeks this kind of recognition, it's worth making the effort to learn how you can contribute to the process. Now read on…

Dr Alison Baverstock
Former publisher
Author of a range of titles on marketing in publishing, and Course Leader for MA Publishing at Kingston University
www.alisonbaverstock.com Twitter: @alisonbav

Introduction

Congratulations – You're a Published Author!

Never again will you pick up a book in a library or bookshop and gaze enviously at the author's blurb thinking "That could have been me!" You've achieved what so many people plan all their lives to do, but never accomplish. You've battled the blank page and won. You've published your book.

No doubt you've already distributed copies to your nearest and dearest – and with any luck they'll have told their friends about it too. Unless you have an extraordinarily large extended family and an exceptional network of friends and contacts, you'll still have a lot of copies unsold. What you'd really like to see is a queue of avid readers snapping them up in bookshops and ordering them online.

Once you've got over the euphoria of completing your manuscript, securing your publishing deal, checking your proofs, and holding the first printed copy in your hand, it's not unusual to feel a bit flat. It would be easy to disregard the boxes of unsold books stacked up in your spare bedroom and retreat to what you love doing best: writing.

To carry on writing is great – but it would be a shame not to do justice to the merits of your first book by selling as many copies as you can. Sell half of them and you'll probably cover the cost of the first print run. Make a profit and you could pay for the publication of the second edition or next book. Raise your profile as an author while you're doing your promotion and you will have a much greater chance of attracting a mainstream publisher in future (if indeed that's the way you want to go).

Even if you have been lucky enough to have had your first book commissioned by a mainstream publisher, you'll sell more copies if you supplement the publisher's publicity campaign (which probably covers only the bare essentials) by boosting sales yourself.

So how are you going to sell more copies? The answer lies in your hand. Read this book. Do all it recommends to give your book the best chance of selling more copies. Even if you put only some of its recommendations into practice, you'll be much more likely to regain your spare bedroom – and secure yourself greater success and respect as a serious author. You'll learn new skills, meet interesting people, visit new places – and you'll almost certainly enjoy yourself along the way!

1

Must I?

Why You Should Promote Your Book

The path of least resistance is the path of the loser.
HG Wells

Any new author who tells you he has never fantasised about his book becoming a bestseller isn't being entirely honest. Of *course* every author wants a bestseller on his or her hands!

But what makes a bestseller? Brilliant writing? An original style? An intriguing plot? Profound truths? Stunning cover design?

To get some pointers, I studied a list of the UK's bestselling books one Christmas[1]. It threw up some telling facts and figures. Of the twenty-five top titles:

- TEN were written by people famous for something other than writing books and who had long-standing substantial personal publicity campaigns behind everything they do (e.g. celebrity chef, comedian, actor).

- FIVE were spin-offs from a successful TV or radio programme.

- TWO were not written by individual authors but were compiled by long-standing national institutions, promoted

[1] Best Sellers, *The Times*, Saturday 1 January 2011

all year, every year (*Guinness Book of World Records, Beano Annual*).

- TWO were books promoted by the Richard and Judy WH Smith Book Club.

- NONE were by authors I'd never heard of.

The top seller was the latest cookery book by Jamie Oliver, the highest profile celebrity chef in the country. A long-running, high-cost publicity machine of many years' duration has made him a household name, guaranteed to gain attention whatever he does. Even so, whenever he brings out a new book, his publisher undertakes a major publicity campaign including expensive national advertising, book signings and interviews.

The second book on the list was, to my surprise, a spin-off from a much-loved TV advertisement for insurance. Thousands and thousands of pounds have been spent on the TV campaign. Really the book is an inventive form of extended advertising, packaged and promoted in time for the Christmas market. It will have found itself in many stockings alongside a toy meerkat. No-one can see the cover without recalling the name of the insurance company and its slogan – the hallmark of a successful advert. Great literature it most certainly is not (though it's had more than 100 five star reviews on Amazon) but it *is* brilliant marketing. *Simple.*

Also near the top of the list was another household name: Stephen Fry. You might think that with his extensive film, TV and radio appearances and in other roles – game show host, comedian, actor, traveller – this national treasure would not need to promote his books at all, but he does. His publisher organises endless national book signing tours and he seems to appear at just about every literature festival in the country. He is a brilliant live speaker: I have seen him at the Cheltenham Literature Festival on sparkling form and he's undeniably charismatic. However he still depends on promotion to sell his books in the desired quantity.

These media megastars are selling tens of thousands of books every week. Their promotional budget is funded by the mainstream publishers who produce their books in return for a substantial profit.

You, by contrast, may not have any commitment to publicity from your publisher (nor should you expect it), other than perhaps listing your book in an online shop or providing promotional materials (at your expense), if you request them. If you want more marketing support, you will be expected to pay for it.

If you think that a publisher's profit from producing your book should cover its marketing costs, think again. We're not just talking about the print costs of a few posters and bookmarks. Promoting a book is very, very time-consuming, involving many hours of work with no guarantee of success. Although for the bulk of the work, the cost is simply an individual's time, rather than material expenses, a publisher's manpower means wages.

You may decide to earn enough money another way to fund a PR person's wages. (That's the attitude I've taken to my housework for years!) Bear in mind that a good book marketing campaign will take many hours over many weeks and will never really end. Take on these tasks yourself (and this book will help you to do that), and your time will cost you nothing.

It's not even all about money – because a publishing company doesn't exist that could field a person more passionate about your writing than you. If you want to find the best ambassador in the world for your book, to speak with unparalleled passion, expertise and intimate knowledge, for free, any time of the day or night, whatever the weather, *look in the mirror!* I think you've just got yourself a job...

Feeling daunted? Please don't! The good news is that your sales target will be much smaller than Stephen Fry's and the scope of your task will be much more modest. Your print run probably numbers in hundreds rather than thousands. Assuming that your book is not utter drivel and that it's not on such a specialised subject that your potential audience is smaller than your print run, selling all these copies will not be such a tall order, provided you employ an intelligent and appropriate promotional strategy. Many tactics exist that cost little or nothing except your time and concentration, not unlike the writing of your book. These activities will also help you gain perspective on your book and enable you to make your next book (if you plan one) even better.

Before looking in detail at the promotional options open to you, it is worth taking time to examine the modern market for books so that you will feel confident and informed about the context in which you will be operating. This will be summarised in the next chapter.

2

Who Will Buy?

The Modern Market for Books

Failure is not an option.
Gene Kranz, Flight Director, in the film *Apollo 13*

It's hard not to feel disheartened as yet another high street bookstore puts up its "closed" sign for the last time. But never fear – as a writer in the digital age, you have far more opportunities to sell your books than any previous generation. The marketplace is not diminishing but evolving. To exorcise any fear of failure, let's put these market changes into perspective. First, the bad news...

Houston, We Have A Problem

Many high street book retailers are having a hard time. Not only have a lot of small independent traders disappeared from the high street, but also some large, established chains have been struggling. Only a few years ago, the US success story Borders hit UK shores. They brought comfortable in-store coffee shops. They installed sumptuous sofas on which to linger over potential purchases. These innovations encouraged shoppers to increase their dwell-time in bookshops, visit more frequently and spend much more. If any bookshop chain could succeed, surely this one would. It could even have revitalised our high street book trade, already flagging before the arrival of the e-book. But in 2011, Borders fizzled out into administration, its mission failed.

What went wrong? It seems the modern book buyer had defected to other sources, partly for convenience, partly for price:

- Most supermarkets now stock an extremely limited but heavily discounted book range, carefully chosen to match their shoppers' profiles.

- Mushrooming online giants such as Amazon offer 24-hour ordering facilities, huge stocks, and often free next-day delivery, pandering to the instant gratification expected by the modern consumer.

- Schools distribute children's publishers' catalogues to target families directly, offering attractive incentives for participating institutions.

- Catalogue traders, both online and offline, offer a limited range at prices hugely discounted by the publishers in return for guaranteed volume sales.

- The ubiquitous franchised man-with-a-van tours workplaces and schools with equally tempting offers (great news for the chosen few authors listed, but an avenue not open to many).

- Slick remainder retailers mop up overstocked titles rejected by the big chains.

- Specialist charity bookshops recycle second-hand items – irresistible sources of cut-price reading matter for the book-lover on a budget, but offering no financial return for the author.

To remain viable and profitable against all of this competition, the conventional high street bookseller has to be very smart and very charming.

Meanwhile the other great British reading resource, the public library, is under threat. Local councils tasked with hard-pruning their budgets are trying to close smaller, less-used libraries. This will inevitably reduce the purchase of books for public lending and the opportunity for readers to try a book which they may then go on to buy.

Amid this tumult of change, most publishers are becoming more risk-averse. It is very rare indeed to hear of large advances paid to new authors (and if we do hear of them, they've only hit the headlines because they are so unusual). Most commissioning editors are prepared to take on only established authors who are a very safe bet. A runaway bestseller can fund the balance of a publisher's list for the rest of the year. However, only top-performing publishers with the judgement and buying power to sign up bestsellers and celebrities will take a chance on a new and unknown author. Advances to unknown authors, and even reasonable returns to established ones, are becoming increasingly rare.

As a result, only a tiny percentage of top-selling authors earn a living from their books. Even for books commissioned by mainstream publishers, the author pockets only about five per cent of the cover price. At this rate, you'd need to sell half a million copies of a typical paperback every year to earn a modest salary. Suddenly that pile of books in your garage may not seem quite so big after all.

Very successful writers may also earn fees for television and radio appearances, merchandising and film rights, features and articles in the press and speaking on the after-dinner speech circuit. But gone are the days when writing books was a self-funding profession, if indeed it ever really was.

It's not that the public has fallen out of love with reading – far from it. It just means its needs are being met in a different way. So let's now see why there's no need to abort your mission to sell your books.

We Have Lift-Off

How many new books do you think are published each year in the UK? The answer is astonishing: in excess of 200,000. Our population is around a fifth of the USA's, but we publish four-fifths as many books as they do each year. We are a book-hungry nation. (Be thankful you're not writing in Oman: it sits at the bottom of the league table for book publishing with just seven new titles per year![2])

In the UK, reading has never been as high profile or as fashionable as it is now. Recent governments have been raising the profile of literacy ever higher and introducing many schemes to promote reading, such as making Literacy Hour a daily requirement in primary schools nationwide[3]. Independent charities such as BookStart[4] and Read for Good[5] supplement and complement government policy. These persuasive schemes promote reading in leisure time, encouraging children to develop a lifelong love of reading and to reap the many educational, social and personal benefits it is proven to bring. Commercial publishers combine forces globally to run high profile promotions for children and adults. World Book Day has been long established for children and the new World Book Night for adults was launched in 2011. These initiatives

[2] Source: Wikipedia – http://en.wikipedia.org/wiki/Books_published_per_country_per_year
[3] Source: The National Literacy Trust http://www.literacytrust.org.uk/reading_connects/resources/331_the_literacy_hour_in_primary_schools
[4] http://www.bookstart.org.uk/about-us/about-booktrust/
[5] http://www.readathon.org

ensure that reading is constantly in the public eye long after the end of an individual's formal education.

One Giant Leap for Mankind

Advances in print technology have made the publication of new books easier. Digital printing has become commonplace, providing a simpler, faster and more flexible printing option than older methods. In traditional offset printing, the image is copied from specially produced plates. A different plate is required for each page and every colour, and changing the plates is very labour intensive. Digital printing does not use plates, generating the image instead from files stored electronically. (Did you realise that when you print out your manuscript on your inkjet or laser printer at home, you are using digital printing?)

Digital technology makes shorter print runs more cost-effective than offset, both in black-and-white and colour. This is a big benefit for the self-funding author. You do not have to commit to such a large print run. With a more realistic number to sell, you have a greater chance of covering your costs. You may even opt for Print on Demand (POD). Here you pay upfront for the set-up costs of the electronic file, but then only print and pay for copies as you need them – perhaps twenty at a time, or even one at a time if that's what you need. (If you've ever seen adverts for personalised books for children, featuring your child's name as the hero or heroine, and wondered how they are produced, digital Print on Demand is the answer.) Although Print on Demand commands a higher price per item, at least you know you'll sell every copy you produce or rather, you only produce a copy once you know you've sold it. This way, you'll never have to worry about where to store surplus copies. Remember this: a printer will tell you that if printing 500 books for £1000, they cost you £2 each – but if you sell only 100 of them, they've actually cost you £10 each in real terms. Bad news if you've set a cover price of £9.99!

Offset is still used for printing very large runs, such as mainstream bestsellers, because it works out cheaper per page and per book, but in time it is expected that digital printing will match and even surpass the cost benefits of offset.

The Rise of the E-Reader

The advent of the e-reader brings further digital benefits. E-readers are small, portable storage devices for e-books, which are books in electronic form. They are lighter and slimmer than paperbacks, and more robust. (One recent advert shows a lady smiling indulgently as her dog licks her e-reader!)

Competitive development has given rise to ever-smarter, ever-cheaper products that are notching up astonishing sales figures. Seasonal advertising has turned them into top Christmas sellers as the ultimate gift for the book-lover who has everything. Using an e-reader, you can read a book without ever touching a printed page. Those accustomed to downloading music and podcasts on electronic gadgets find it a natural progression to buy their reading material this way, and for the younger generation the process makes reading seem cool. The latest e-readers, with integral wireless internet connectivity, make it possible to download entire books at a moment's notice. This facility for instant gratification encourages more impulse buys and more frequent purchasing – or so the publishers hope. (I know that since I've bought mine, I've read a lot more books than I would have done otherwise, many of them spur-of-the-moment purchases.)

You can also download free samples of many e-books to try before you buy. At the end of the free sample, up pops the option to buy the whole book at the list price – especially tempting if the sample ends on a cliff-hanger!

Interestingly, the rise of the e-reader has also fuelled huge interest in of out-of-copyright classics, available free of charge.

The E-Book and the Online Book

Serving these e-readers is an increasing quantity of e-books, most of which are simply electronic versions of conventionally published books. The jury is out on e-book pricing. Some authors and publishers set their e-book prices only slightly below the price of the print edition, while others price low to attract new readers. Many authors with more than one e-book to their name will periodically offer one of them as a free download, hoping to hook satisfied readers who will then be happy to buy the rest of them at full price.

It's also an option to publish books solely for the e-reader, avoiding the cost of traditional print altogether. What a gift for hard-up self-funders!

Even before the emergence of the e-reader, some writers had already decided to publish their books online, posting them up on websites or blogs. Some charged readers for access, others requested donations. Many simply allowed free viewing, content to have readers without the trouble of following the conventional publishing route. Most bloggers fall into this last category.

While for some people, free online publishing is enough to satisfy their authorly ambitions without incurring costs, for others e-books have been the overture to a conventional, mainstream publishing career. Yes, it can be done! American writer Amanda Hocking's clever strategy with e-books, priced low and backed by extensive use of social media (and, of course, a page-turning product) led to a bidding war between mainstream publishers eager to sign her to a seven figure contract. (Visit her website, www.amandahocking.net for inspiration.)

Publishing exclusively in electronic form limits the availability of a book to those with the right technology. But even those with very limited financial resources can engage and connect with readers online.

Not all booklovers embrace the new technology. The children's electronic market is still very small, perhaps because parents are reluctant or unable to fund e-readers for their kids or worry that they'll be used only for gaming. Conversely, tentative attempts to launch books on top-selling handheld game consoles have been half-hearted, limiting packages to out-of-copyright classics: I suspect their manufacturers are more comfortable and more optimistic about the profitability of games than of e-books. To grow this market, children's publishers are developing e-book technology that will allow physically interactive reading experiences offered by many modern classic children's books, such as Eric Carle's *The Very Hungry Caterpillar.*

Among adults, there are many who prefer the tactile experience of traditional books – browsing in bookshops and libraries, stroking the covers, insisting that books furnish a room. But as e-reader prices continue to fall, it's likely that more will succumb to at least using both formats, if not actually preferring the e-book.

Personally, I'm torn. I love the physicality of books – the smell of the paper, the rustle of the page, the technical small print naming the font that it's set in. I know I'm not alone in this passion: when he was small, my nephew used to draw meticulous barcodes on the toy books he made. He's now a professional librarian.

However, I also embrace the portability of the electronic device. Before the advent of the e-reader, I snapped up its forerunner, a game chip for the Nintendo DS, called 100 Classic Books. I marvelled at the ability for such a tiny device to store the complete works of Dickens, Austen and others within the confines of my handbag. It was fantastic for travelling or while in hospital.

My family succumbed to the Christmas advertising campaign and now we're a two-Kindle household, with a few children's books loaded onto mine for my daughter too. My husband keeps his in his pocket, mine is always in my handbag, and this creates more reading opportunities when we're on the move. I've downloaded plenty of free e-books but I've also gone on to buy hard copies of e-books that I've enjoyed so that I can physically have them on my already loaded bookshelves. I like to flick through real books and re-read them and pass them on to friends with a recommendation. For me, old and new technology work hand-in-hand, increasing my volume of reading and creating more sales opportunities for authors.

I still buy most of my books second-hand in charity bookshops. I often splash out and buy books I don't really need on the basis that the money goes to a good cause. As yet, there's no charity shop equivalent for e-books, so digital technology will not yet turn my book-cluttered house into a Zen zone any time soon, but maybe that will change. After all, libraries are already facilitating e-book lending, and who knows what the future might bring? Whether you prefer old or new book technology, there is no denying that as far as publishing is concerned, we live in very exciting times.

Like me, many book-buyers have room in their lives for both old and new technology. As an author, ignore either group at your peril!

Self-Publishing Comes of Age
Before all this technology came along, the only resort of authors rejected by mainstream commercial publishing houses was to turn to what were disparagingly known as "vanity

publishers". These companies were happy to take your money (and usually a lot of it) to turn your manuscript into a printed, bound book, adding little or no guidance to improve its merit. Thanks in part to the advantages offered by the latest technology, they are being superseded by more professional publishing consultants who offer a host of expert services to refine your manuscript and make it commercially viable. They will almost certainly have their own web presence and are highly experienced in all the new technologies as well as old-fashioned print. You may well find yourself doing a satisfactory deal entirely over the internet, exchanging manuscripts and proofs as electronic files and never having the joy of telling your friends, "I'm just off to lunch with my publisher!" The best service will come from those able to offer a personal service, with substantial customer contact by email and by phone, even if you never meet them face-to-face.

Power to the Author!

For the new author, all of these developments are very empowering. It has never been cheaper or easier to publish a book, to gain professional and impartial advice and to promote it before the whole world. Cheaper and easier for you – but also for your competition! So how are you, as the newly published author, going to make your mark within that vast marketplace?

You will need a strategic campaign that focuses on the segment of the market most receptive to your book. You must identify your target readers, get their attention, win their interest and desire and make it as easy as possible for them to buy your book.

Does that sound scary? Well, it won't be if you break down the process into small and manageable steps. The following chapters will demonstrate how to do just that. You can carry out these activities in your own time, at a pace that suits you and that fits in around the rest of your life. They will work for you whether you are a full-time employee writing as a hobby, a part-time juggler of work, home and family or in the fortunate position of being able to devote all your waking hours and energies to your publishing ambitions.

But first you're going to have to get yourself organised! The next chapter will show you how.

3

Action Stations

Planning Your Campaign

The longest journey starts with a single step.
Lao Tzu – Chinese Philosopher

While you were writing your book, you probably dreamed at some point of signing published copies in a busy bookshop with a queue of eager fans waiting to exchange a few words with you as you write their dedication. That may happen yet. Even for bestselling authors whose books are published commercially, this never happens without serious commitment, strategic planning and a lot of hard work behind the scenes from many people, not least the author.

Amelia Fairney, Publicity Director at Penguin Books (General), provides some perspective:

> The author needs to realise that they are as responsible as the publisher for getting out there and selling their book – whether that means bookshop talks, writing for newspapers, radio interviews, blogging, etc. I also think that every serious writer needs a good website that they run themselves and update on a daily basis.

Self-published thriller writer Shaun Ivory concurs, drawing on over ten years of novel-writing experience:

No matter how much time you spend on your book, the onus is on you to sell it. You must get this fixed in your head and keep it there. You will forget, but sales and falling interest will remind you! The easiest part is the writing.

Shaun should know: after much hard graft, he successfully sold the entire first print run of 200 of his first novel, *The Judas Cup*, and then went on to a smaller second print run.

If this is not what you wanted to hear, don't panic: the challenge is not as insurmountable as it sounds. Like most complex tasks, the project of promoting your book will be much more manageable if you break it down into many smaller steps.

Plan your campaign as if it were your summer holiday. If you decide where you want to go before you set off, you'll have a much better chance of ending up in the place you want to be, at a price you can afford – and of having an appropriately packed suitcase when you get there.

Name Your Goal

Planning is key. At the very beginning, ask yourself lots of questions to make sure you're heading in the right direction. The most important is this first one: what would have to happen to make you sit down at the end of your book promotion and say you are happy? Then aim for that result.

There is no set pattern which you are obliged to follow. What's right for you may not be right for someone else. Assuming you're self-published, the book is *your* project, funded by *you,* and *you* are calling the shots. If your main objective in producing a printed book of your poetry is just to give it to your family and friends as something to remember you by, additional sales may not matter. But if you want to become a well-known and successful author beyond your social sphere, you will need to do much more.

Richard Denning, the ambitious and energetic author of a series of historical fantasy books for young adults, has the cool and clinical approach to marketing that you might expect from a writer whose day job is in the medical profession.

"I deliberately *did not* target friends, relations, colleagues or neighbours because I wanted my books to sell on their own merits to people I did not know," he says.

Although this is a tough line to follow, his strategy is paying off.

You don't have to be as hard on yourself as Richard – but you are the person who has most to gain or lose here, so don't sell yourself short. Cultivate the habits of the opportunist: create your own luck. Be on the lookout for chances to promote your book and yourself at every turn, and follow your dream.

Get Real

At all times, be realistic about what you can achieve with what you have to work with. Consider not only your book, but the sort of person that you are and your available time, money and other resources. Take time to think about the following questions and answer them honestly before you get down to the practical scheduling of promotional events and activities. Jot down your answers to clarify your thoughts and you'll have the starting point of a formal marketing plan.

- Do you simply want to cover your costs, or do you seek fame at any cost, even if it means spending more than you'll earn from book sales?

- How many copies are you prepared to give away as review copies, as sprats to catch the mackerel?

- Are you happy to reveal your identity in public, or do you want to protect your privacy?

- Are you comfortable meeting new people and talking to them about your book, e.g. in libraries or bookshops at book signings and literary festivals?

- Are you prepared to talk to your readers about what it's been like to write your book? If so, which age group is appropriate – children or adults?

- How much time can you spare each day/week/month to invest in publicity for your book?

- How much effort and energy are you prepared to put into promotion?

Having thought all that through, keep your answers to hand. You're now ready to move on to identifying your target market.

4

Stake Your Claim!

Identifying Your Market

Know Thyself
Inscribed in the Temple of Apollo at Delphi, home of the famous Oracle

Before you start promoting your book, you need to be clear about exactly who you are targeting. To do this, you need to identify and categorise your book. For this you must distance yourself from it as its author, and this may not be easy or obvious: it's like asking a parent to be objective about their child.

A good first question to ask is: where would it sit in a bookshop or library? Browse round both to see in which section yours would naturally belong.

Depending on the nature of your book, this may be a very simple definition. If you've written a handbook for stamp collectors there will be special interest websites, magazines and groups that you may target. If your book is aimed solely at children who are taking up the hobby for the first time, you may wish to target children's websites, magazines, schools and clubs rather than preaching to the converted who have already progressed way beyond that level.

If your book has a broader appeal – for example, it's a chick-lit novel or a thriller – there are so many means of reaching the potential reader, it will be hard to know where to start. Cast your net too widely and you will over-reach yourself in terms of time and spend, while still not making a dent in such a vast marketplace. It doesn't mean that the wider market might not be interested in due course, but you need first to get a foothold on this vast mountain. If you can first create a loyal following in your local area, for example, or within your profession, you'll have a firmer launching pad for the trajectory of your writing career.

Beware of getting diverted in the wrong direction because of superficial similarities. MC Beaton and Ian Rankin both write crime novels set in Scotland, but they appeal to very different readerships; one gentle and humorous, the other harsh and gritty. Call yourself Blackpool's answer to Jilly Cooper because you're aiming at the chick-lit genre, and your readers will be bitterly disappointed if you don't include raunchy sex-scenes. If you want to compare yourself to an established author, make sure you choose one that is appropriate to your work.

Don't aim at too broad of a group. This is known in the advertising trade as "wastage", i.e. people you've paid to reach but who aren't really interested in your product. Consider for a moment the commercial world of television advertising. Imagine you are a food manufacturer trying to boost sales of a new gourmet cooking oil on a fixed budget. Would you really just aim for as many viewers as possible without selecting who they were? Would you buy a slot during the programme with the highest viewing figures? No, you'd opt for ad breaks in a carefully chosen programme, probably to do with cookery, where it would be seen by far fewer people, but who would be cooking enthusiasts in the frame of mind to think about culinary products. Bigger is not always better, no more than highest cost means best value.

It might also be helpful to think back to your school maths lessons about the concept of sets. Within the vast potential marketplace of people who buy books, there are many subsets of readers. If you've written a book aimed exclusively at women, these sets include married women, single women, widows, career women, retired women, new mothers, diabetic women, women who married foreigners; the list is endless. Only a small number of these sets – maybe as few as one – should be targeted by your promotion. The more specific you can be about the description of who you want to reach, the more success you will have. Try to define your target market as precisely as you can. The more particular you are, the more appropriately targeted your marketing can be, and the greater your chances of sales.

Let's look at two examples of self-published books that might at first seem to be in the same sector: motoring.

First up is *Corvette Racing – The GT1 Years* by Nigel S Dobbie. "Ah," you might think. "A book about cars." Motoring interest, maybe (being sexist here) for men; something to promote as an ideal Christmas present for that oh-so-difficult-to-buy-for uncle who's keen on motor racing? Then you look at the price tag: a cool £60! The only book I possess that cost that much is a vast two-volume Oxford English Dictionary and I don't expect ever to pay that much for a single book again. But Nigel S Dobbie's book, though costly, is large format, full colour, superbly written, well marketed (by himself) to his small but substantial special interest group, and his first print run sold out within a year of publication. His readers post rave reviews about what a fabulous book it is, testifying that it is great value for money, and his second print run is selling steadily.

Let's take another book about motoring, this time by Professor William Fairney: *Richard Stephens and The Clevedon Motor Cars*, cover price £13.95. This one is aimed at quite a different market: the vintage collector, the technical boffin and the local populace of Clevedon, where this innovative car design came into being. Now that would make a good Christmas present for my brother-in-law, who likes cars and history and comes from Clevedon! This book continues to sell some years after publication, fuelled by Bill's active marketing programme.

So although both of these books are broadly in the motoring sector, as are many others, from the *Haynes Manual* series to *The Highway Code*, you would clearly need to go about promoting these two books in very different ways. Do not let yourself be fooled by superficial similarities, nor should you be lazy and simply mimic what has been done for another book that sounds similar to your own.

For some books, defining and reaching the market is easy. For Nigel S Dobbie, himself a passionate fan of Corvette racing, his market is clear cut: those who share his passion. It's a relatively small market but a dedicated one which includes many fans for whom his £60 cover price is a bargain and who have responded with rave reviews. It's not hard to identify and track them down because by definition they'll attend relevant racing events, and Nigel has sold many of his books by taking them to race meetings. There's also a Corvette Museum dedicated to this sport which was pleased to stock his book. For those he can't meet in person, he has an established new media network including a website and a presence on Facebook and other social media.

For other authors' books, the task is much harder. When Indian author G D Kokani published his philosophical work on the human condition, *Human Nature*, it was hard to know where to begin. Surely every potential reader shares the human condition? Careful planning of a blog tour of readers and reviewers interested in similar books is helping him home in on a realistic target.

For your book, start by defining a small but specific group of the people who are the most likely to be persuaded to buy. Think accurate, targeted shots as opposed to scattergun fire. Plan a marketing strategy to saturate that sector and then move on to the next most likely subset. If you can reach and satisfy a small core of closely matched readers naturally predisposed to your work, you should find their influence radiates outwards to others by personal recommendation and word-of-mouth. Once you have focused on exactly which tiny subset of the vast market for books you are aiming at, it is time to examine that marketplace more closely to determine how to raise your book's profile within it. But just before we proceed in that direction...

Don't Forget the Writer

Before we delve into the nature of your reader, let's home in for a moment on a more important person: *you*, its author.

You may feel that you as a person are irrelevant; surely people are buying what you've written, not who you are? Your product is not only the book that you have published, it's also yourself. There are almost certainly some key factors about you that will increase people's interest in your book.

If you've written a novel based inside a cosmetic surgery hospital, your professional qualifications and career as a cosmetic surgery theatre nurse will add conviction and credibility to your marketing material. You could offer interesting interviews about how your career inspired your book, and you may also target the professional nursing press. Would James Herriot have sold so many books if he hadn't told the world he was a vet?

Conversely, if your background has nothing to do with the target market sector for your book, the contrast might be a point of interest. A few pages ago, weren't you intrigued by the GP who writes escapist fantasy? Equally, I was drawn to find out more about a serious academic who writes about fairies (Paul Newnton). Such details are like gold dust in any PR campaign. No journalist is looking for a headline that says "Self-published author published a book" (remember, with 200,000 books being published every year in the UK, the fact of publication is not a unique and interesting story). But a journalist may be interested in the story *behind* the story, so that's what you need to tell him. His resulting feature will then help you sell your book.

Whatever else your claim to fame, there will be at least one geographical territory in which you will be newsworthy as a local author. As a reader, don't you feel more of a bond with an author who comes from your hometown or county? If you lived next door to an author, went to school with one or shared an office with one in their day job, wouldn't you be more likely to read their books? You'd also be more likely to mention them to anyone you know who is keen on that genre.

My father was in the same primary school class as the former Children's Laureate Quentin Blake. (He now wishes he'd kept the cartoons his friend sketched of their headmaster!) This tenuous connection has made my family follow Quentin Blake's career with a special interest, and between us, we must have bought dozens of his books over the years.

My daughter is at school with the son of Caroline Mockford, who produces gorgeous, vividly illustrated books about Cleo the Cat. If ever I want to buy a book for a young child, hers are my first choice – not least because it's easy to nip down the road to get them autographed!

This may seem superficial, but personal associations like this really do work in your favour, so don't hesitate to milk them while you are getting yourself established. Many famous authors have done the same.

There may be other territories in which you can be newsworthy. Author Jill Rutherford, originally from Wales, wrote a book about her travels in Japan. She now lives in Sussex where she launched her promotional campaign. The fact that she is a local resident captured the attention of the local press (not least because of her determined promotional campaign). She gave advance readings of her book at local festivals, she networks effectively with the local Waterstones to run book signing events, and she invited the Mayor of Eastbourne as guest of honour to her book launch. Photos of her well-attended launch party add credibility to her website. Great reviews from local readers are helping her to gain readers from further afield. She is now in a much stronger position to promote her book to larger, more distant markets.

Like Jill, think of your chosen territory as your comfort zone and a safe rehearsal ground. Work this audience well and you will gain confidence to perform before a wider audience.

And now it's time to home in on your target reader within that territory...

5

Dear Reader

Getting to Know Your Target Audience

The human race, to which so many of my readers belong.
GK Chesterton

Once you have identified a small and specific initial target market for your first promotional efforts, try to build up an accurate profile of what this group of potential readers is like. If you're a novelist, this will be a similar exercise to creating a character. The more closely you can identify your target group, the easier it will be for you to promote your book. Think of yourself as a stalker – in the nicest possible way!

Think laterally. Have a brainstorm with supportive, interested friends and jot down everything you can think of that would enable you to engage with this group of people. Don't reject any suggestions straight off, but let them brew for a bit.

Work out where you can most easily reach them. You want to try to catch their attention not only when they're in a book-buying frame of mind but also when they are engaged in other pursuits. These may or may not be related to your book. To kick off, ask yourself these questions:

* What is your target reader like at home?

* What kind of home do they live in – and do they live alone or in a family group?

- Which papers do they read, which television programmes do they like, what other books do they read?

- Where do they usually buy their books?

- Do they use the local library?

- Are they keen users of the internet and other new media?

- What hobbies might they pursue?

- Where do they go when not at home – school, work, leisure groups, social activities?

- If your book is about a very specialised interest, where does your target reader indulge in that interest?

- Are there specialist events, meetings or institutions that they might go to?

- Are they likely to be influenced by any other group of people you might target?

Let's take as an example a self-help book for new mothers. This is a huge, nationwide and ever-present market, so it's not surprising that lots of other books are already available to this group. How will you make yours stand out? Your answers to the questions posed above might be:

- Living in a family group maybe with one or more children already.

- If living alone as single parents, arguably more likely

to need the support of a self-help book (though less likely to have the disposable income to buy their own copy).

- May or may not be employed (but in the short-term on maternity leave).

- Could take any newspaper but likely currently to read parenting magazines or parenting features in the press.

- Regular visitor to GP's surgery or clinic.

- Heavily influenced by practice nurses, health visitors and other clinic staff.

- Possibly involved in local NCT (National Childbirth Trust) classes.

- Regular customer of supermarket and pharmacy.

- Target customer of any specialist baby supplies shops and toyshops.

- Possible customer of local photographers specialising in babies or family groups.

- Probably in a local network of like-minded, similar-aged new mums.

- Might attend mother-and-baby/toddler/child groups.

- Could be interested in local sales for that age group e.g. NCT events.

- Possibly in local primary school network for older children.

- May well be keen internet users subscribing to popular parenting websites.

From this list emerges a mass of tangible, realistic promotional opportunities to reach this target audience. Though the market is potentially nationwide (unless you live in the middle of nowhere), a little extra research will turn these ideas into concrete local opportunities. For example:

- Offer a free talk and book signing for mums at the local library or bookshop to coincide with...

- Scheduled story sessions for toddlers.

- Approach the editor of the women's page in the local paper(s) to suggest an interview.

- Target the local NCT's membership publication.

- Get your blog listed on the Mumsnet bloggers' forum.

- Offer to give a talk to your local clinics, NCT groups and mother-and-baby groups.

- Take a stall at local NCT sales and nursery or primary school events.

- Offer free copies to local midwives, health visitors and support groups for single parents on the condition that they distribute promotional bookmarks or vouchers to be handed out to those they meet.

- Offer to hold a book signing event at the local branch of Mothercare or baby section of Boots.

- Set up a special promotional deal with local baby photographers.

And so on...Conquering the local market with a task list like this will put you in a much stronger position to promote your book further afield, perhaps with national parenting magazines. You might even sell out your initial print run without needing to go any further. You could then print a second batch to promote further afield – or indeed to continue to target the rolling population of new mums in your area. (This is a *great* market because, wherever you live, there will always be more new mums every year!)

On the other hand, your target market may be very small and limited, because that's what matches your book. I've been involved in the production of a series of history books about the small Cotswold village of Hawkesbury Upton (population 1,200). The book will never make the pages of *The Times Literary Supplement, History Today* or even *Cotswold Life* – but for those who have connections with this tiny catchment area, it is compulsive reading and an heirloom. At its launch, good reviews were secured in the small local paper and parish magazine, both ideal means of reaching its target readers. The modest launch event, hosted in the village hall, the focal point of community life and totally appropriate for its target audience, cost next to nothing. Yet within two months of publication, handily scheduled for the run-up to Christmas, it had sold 400 copies. It not only covered its costs, but generated a healthy profit, donated by the authors to local village causes. With this track record, the authors can be confident that any future volumes they produce will be well received. This project was small in the global world of publishing but a stunning success in its own terms. If your market is small but you saturate it, you can want for no more.

Even if your book may have wider appeal, it's always worth focusing first on those most likely to be interested in your particular book – those who work in the industry it describes, for example, or who live in the area in which it's set. Self-published thriller writer Shaun Ivory, whose first book was set in his home country of Ireland, sold out of his initial print run solely by promoting it within that country.

When you've conquered your comfort zone, head further afield and aim at building your empire. If you are exceptionally clever and lucky, your localised success might even attract the attention of a mainstream publisher.

So, now you've decided who and where your first target readers are, don't race off to begin promoting your book to them just yet. Before you do that, you need to think a little more about *you*. You, the author, must have a profile and a presence. And the focal point for that should be online...

6

The Truth is Out There!

Harnessing the Internet

The Internet is becoming the town square
for the global village of tomorrow.
Bill Gates

Thanks to the internet, the twenty-first century is a golden age of opportunity for the self-published author. Never has it been easier to promote your book to a truly global audience than via the wonder that is the world-wide web.

These days, authors are expected by reporters, retailers and readers to have their own online presence. You *will* be "Googled" – and not just by your mum or your best friend! If a journalist wants to check some facts for a news story about you, the first thing he or she will do is put your name or your book title into a search engine. If a retailer is dithering about whether to stock your book, they may well look for your website to gauge your popularity. Readers who enjoy your first book may want to find out more about the author or to check out whether there's a sequel in the pipeline. They'll expect to find the answers online.

You may already have a limited presence on your publisher's website, where your book may be offered for sale online. Acquiring an ISBN number and registering with Nielsen BookData will have pushed through basic information about your book to retailers who will add it to their stock control systems.

However, the best form of marketing is to have your own online presence in the form of an official website, devoted entirely to you and under your control. A good website compounds your credibility as an author. It gives you a springboard for raising your profile across the rest of the internet and all over the world. If you don't organise your own online presence, your image will be totally at the mercy of anyone else who writes about you online. You can be certain that your competition will be making the most of online promotional opportunities and you should too. So take charge and create your own website as the authorised and authoritative internet source of information about you and your books.

Here are some of the things that people might expect to find on your website:

- An author biography (not a complete CV, but the key points relevant to your book).

- A list of all the books that you have published with dates of publication. (This is especially helpful if you've written a series and people are trying to read them in the right order!)

- A photo of you (not essential but it's nice to put a face to the name).

- A selection of reviews of your books (don't be modest: great reviews will help clinch further sales).

- Sample pages to read before buying (optional but advisable – it may lure in anyone who is reluctant to buy without flicking through first).

- Advance information about new books planned (it's never too soon to start promoting them).

- Regularly updated advance details of any events that you are involved in (e.g. public readings, school visits, appearances at book fairs).

- Any interesting news about you e.g. awards won (they add credibility and audience appeal).

- Your blog (update it frequently to encourage readers to revisit the site).

- An online ordering facility (not everyone likes using Amazon, and you'll get a better mark-up by selling books directly to your readers).

- A contact form for readers to send you messages and reviews (this makes it easy for them to bond with you so they'll want to buy your future books and recommend you to their friends).

There is no medium other than the internet that provides you with the opportunity to have all of these things constantly available, updated as often as you like, around the clock, every day of the year – so make full use of it. If you don't take full advantage, you'll be missing one of the most valuable tricks in the promotional armoury.

If you're already a regular internet user and have set up your own website, this chapter will help you take a fresh look at it to see whether it can work any harder for you. On the other hand, if you're filled with dread at the thought of being seen online, at the potential cost or by your lack of technical know-how, it will allay your fears and help you to catch up with the twenty-first century.

Privacy

Some people hesitate about developing an online presence because they are nervous of infringing their private lives. This doesn't have to be the case. If you write under a pen-name, there is no reason why your real identify has to be revealed online. You can use addresses other than your own for correspondence and despatches, for example your publisher's office or a PO Box. You can set up a separate email address from your private or work one, so that any messages about your book are kept separate and self-contained. You can also use a comment form so that you don't need an email address at all.

Cost

There is no simple answer to how much websites cost, but the good news is that if you tackle it the right way, the price need not be prohibitive. The only reason big commercial organisations spend thousands of pounds on their websites is that their complex needs require custom-written programmes. Consider the brief for the BBC's website, often held up as a model of excellence. It has to cover all of their programming nationwide and make available a vast array of podcasts, children's games and programme trailers, all constantly requiring updating. It must also be possible for viewers to listen/watch live broadcasts or replay recent programmes. A lot of commercial websites include extensive video, sound and special effects to make themselves stand out in a highly competitive marketplace.

In contrast, your website requirements are very simple. So simple, in fact, that you could make a website for nothing!

You don't even have to buy any software. There is plenty of free "open source" software available to download, without the payment of royalties or licence fees. These are a good starting point for the low budget self-published author.

Like email, many of these packages are offered by providers of multiple services keen to engage your loyalty to their brand. Google, for example, offers users of Gmail the chance to develop websites alongside their email package. Some of the most popular services, such as WordPress (www.wordpress.com) and Blogger (www.blogger.com), started as free blogging software systems but now enable you to provide multi-page websites, optionally centred around a blog. Although these need not cost you a penny, you might like to consider some of their chargeable optional extras. For example, for a few pounds a year, you can acquire a website address (also known as a domain name or URL) that doesn't include their standard website suffix, to provide a snappier and more memorable address. You can also take that address with you if you decide to move your website to another system. Any WordPress address remains forever the property of WordPress.

Other services, such as Vistaprint (www.vistaprint.co.uk), offer free hosting only for very small websites, but charge you a monthly fee for larger sites, on a sliding scale as you increase your website's size and with additional charges for optional extras.

Of course, what these providers count on is that many users, once comfortable with the software, will choose to pay for more features and sophistication. That is how these companies remain economically viable. It's entirely up to you which route you want to take.

Another way in which these services are funded is by including advertising either on the software that you see, or on your website itself. It's possible to harness this advertising to generate an income for yourself, according to how many people view your website. If you register with these services, you may get paid a tiny amount per hit that your site generates for the advert. Generally speaking, you'll only make a significant income this way if you have a phenomenally popular website. We're talking about thousands of daily hits here, which is way beyond the reach of most self-published writers' websites. Some writers steer away from advertising of this sort, as it can be distracting or downright annoying for visitors. Always consider your readers and their viewpoint. Would you want to spend much time on a site that had pop-up banners or flashing adverts? If not, then you might think it's worth paying extra to make your site an ad-free zone.

That's just one example of a chargeable extra. Another example is to have more freedom to design your own site. Free software systems usually come with a wide range of different templates and colourways, so that you have a reasonably wide choice of acceptable design formats. If you use them as they are, there's no extra design charge; but supposing you want to make your own page more distinctive to match your book's branding, adding a typeface or colour that doesn't come as standard, you will have to pay extra. It's a bit like choosing a new car – have one with standard fittings and there's no extra cost, but have it customised and it will cost a little more. It's up to you to decide whether those extra benefits are worth the additional investment. Again, many perfectly good websites are built on standard templates, so there's no need to spend much if you don't have the budget or the desire.

Technology
With a can-do attitude and a little application, even the novice can master some of these systems reasonably easily using free online tutorials, help pages and support forums. If you're not

comfortable or confident attempting this on your own, do not think for a moment of engaging a website company more used to working in the commercial sector. Most of these have a starting price of some thousands of pounds without any guarantee of selling a single book for you. Instead seek out the services of a company or freelance designer to set up your basic site. Then pay them a monthly retainer to keep it up to date for you. Alternatively you could get someone to set it up and train you to maintain it yourself, once it's up and running. (I provide both of these services to a number of self-published authors to their satisfaction.) Your publisher may be able to put you in touch with an appropriate person. Another low-cost option would be to sign up for an evening class to learn the basics and gain some confidence at an easily digestible pace. (You might also befriend some potential book-buyers in the process!)

Choosing a URL (website address)

One of the earliest and most important decisions you will have to make about your website is what to call it. This is what's known as the domain name or URL (which stands for Universal Resource Locator) and it effectively acts as the address of your website, wherever it is hosted (i.e. wherever the master file of the website is kept). The domain name always begins www. and often ends in .com, .org, .co.uk or something similar. Each of these suffixes was originally intended to indicate the kind of organisation that was using it. For example, .gov was used to represent a government department, .sch a school and .ac an institute of higher education. Country suffixes such as .uk and .nl were obviously were meant to be associated with a particular geographical area, while those without were international (or originating in the USA!) As the number and variety of websites proliferate, more suffixes are being made available, such as .info and .tv. One of the most recent additions is .me, formerly the country suffix for Montenegro, but with obvious popular appeal to English speakers. (I've just bought the URL www.youngbyname.me for my personal website.) As this book goes to press, there are currently applications in process for such exciting new suffixes as .books. Not all of these will be available to the general public, but the choice will continue to grow.

Choose a domain name that is memorable, distinctive and relevant to your work. It should be easy to guess and easy to spell, so if someone can't remember the exact address, they'll still have a good chance of finding it in a search engine. Like any other piece of marketing, it should be legal, decent, honest and truthful.

If you are planning a single book and want the site to be solely about that book, then you might want to use the name of the book in the URL, e.g. www.warandpeace.com. If you're planning many more books, or want to use it to showcase other work than just your books such as journalism or illustration, you might want to focus on your name, e.g. www.leotolstoy.com or indeed your genre, e.g. www.russianepics.com. URLs are unique: only one website with each web address can exist on the internet. To find out whether your preferred name is available, simply input it to a search engine and see what comes up. (Interestingly, www.warandpeace.com is available at the time of writing but someone has nabbed www.leotolstoy.com!)

Most shareware packages, such as WordPress, will include in your initial account set-up process the facility to choose and secure your URL. If not, you will need to go separately to an online domain registry service to buy the licence to use that URL address, which is usually done for multiples of twelve months. There are many different registry services available, all offering slightly different packages and options, but it should cost you no more than about £15 for the first year, which is then renewable. Shop around different service providers until you find one you're comfortable with at an acceptable price. You will need to input your personal contact details so that the registry service can remind you each time your subscription is due for renewal. Put in as much information as you can to ensure you can be tracked down (postal and email addresses, telephone and mobile numbers, etc.). Don't worry, this information will be kept private and won't appear on your website unless you put it there.

Populating your Website

Once you've chosen your domain name and your software, the next thing to do is to choose the design template of your site and start adding content.

If you're using a system that offers you lots of templates, take time to trawl through them and find a design that reflects the style and tone of your book. Your website should be instantly recognisable as the official online home of your book. It doesn't have to match the colour scheme or the typeface – there is, in any case, only a handful of typefaces that are recommended for internet use, to ensure legibility in different browsers – but it should create the right mood and provide a pleasing backdrop to your book jacket. Thus, a self-help book about relaxation techniques might need a template that is soothing and calming, while a thriller may create a feeling of tension and danger with dark, brooding colours.

Use the list given earlier of which items to include in a website as your starting point to develop the content. Put them in a logical order that will be easy for the viewer to navigate. They should be in the sequence that the reader is likely to want to access them. For example, sample pages should come before the facility to order a copy.

Then put yourself in the place of your readers. Write the content in a way that will make sense to them. Maintain a certain amount of distance, possibly writing about you and your book in the third person, so that it comes across as a professional, confident recommendation from a publisher, rather than from an anxious author eager to please a critical audience. You may be desperate for feedback, but don't make that obvious. It's all too easy to come across as needy and amateurish, and this will undermine the reader's belief in you as an accomplished author whose books he or she should buy.

Attracting Visitors to your Site
There are broadly two kinds of visitors that will arrive at your site: those who have been actively looking specifically for you and your book, and those who have been looking for something else but have stumbled across your site via a search engine.

For surfers who are looking for you and your book, even if they don't know your website's domain name, provided they put in your name and title (or an approximation of it), they will probably be taken to your site, unless there's something else out there which is higher profile. If your name is Len Tolstoy and you've written a book called *War and Pets*, I'm afraid that predictive search engines are more likely to throw up Leo and his famous Russian epic as it's something sought out so frequently.

For those who are looking more broadly, e.g. for books in your subject area, make sure you include suitable keywords throughout your site. Keywords are the terms that readers are most likely to input into search engines when looking for a book like yours, e.g. "travel books about Japan" or "thrillers involving the IRA" to take them to your book. The more often these keywords are mentioned – not only in the body copy of the pages about your book, but also in your domain name, picture captions, alt tags and menu items – the higher your site will rise in the search engines' listings. Beware of overdoing it and sacrificing the flow of your prose for the sake of stuffing in more keywords. Your text should still be readable. If your website reads badly, it suggests that your book is badly written too. Also, if you cheat by adding pages filled only with keywords to lure in the search engines, rumour has it that you may end up blacklisted and the search engines will never show you again! There's a sensible balance to be struck here.

Include a picture of your book cover, so that people will be able to recognise it when they see it in shops. Ideally add a picture of yourself, if you don't mind. (The photo taken for your book jacket's author blurb will do fine and provide continuity.) Use other pictures as appropriate and available. Copyright-free images in the public domain will help you fill empty spaces. Wikipedia is a good source of these.

Don't include too much unbroken copy: big chunks of text on screen are hard on the eye. Readers will quickly tire and click away from your website if you're not careful. In the context of a website, less really is more. Break up the copy with subheadings and graphic devices – little flourishes or lines or empty spaces will do fine. Make the key points jump off the page. People tend to scan web pages rather than read them thoroughly, so make sure the most important points are easy to spot. Eye tracking research proves that people read web pages in an F shape, so make sure the most important points appear within that part of the page. Keep each page short, because people also tire of constantly scrolling down a screen to see more. If a section is running too far down the page, consider whether it really ought to be divided up across more than one page.

Keeping your Website Up to Date

Once you've got the basic information on your website, revisit it every now and again to keep it fresh. Internet search engines are more interested in websites that are frequently updated, even if only by tiny tweaks. Quite reasonably, they consider ever-changing sites to be more important than those that are left untouched.

Include a contact form inviting your readers to submit their reviews to you online. Then every time you get a good review from a reader, add it to your reviews page (with their permission – or anonymously if they don't want their name included). Even if people already post reviews on sites such as Amazon and GoodReads, you should still reproduce the best ones here. (By the way, don't worry if you get a duff review on Amazon – many people disregard the one-star reviews, especially if they seem to have been written by madmen with a chip on their shoulder. They're just as suspect, to my mind, as a five-star review that sounds like it's been written by the author's proud mum.) Conversely, every time you get a fantastic review from someone you know, do your best to persuade them to post it also on Amazon, where the whole world will see it – and where it will help boost your ranking in the Amazon search engine.

Dream up news stories to add, such as the announcement of your book launch (and then after it's happened, a photo-led story reporting on how it went), selling out of your first print run, signing up a new local stockist. Give your website a topical edge by commenting on items related to your genre that are currently in the news.

Add links to other relevant websites, such as a library where you're planning to give a talk, and ask the managers of those websites to insert reciprocal links back to yours. The more inbound links your site has, the more highly the search engines will rate it.

Blogs

Particularly flexible and useful for expanding website content is the act of writing a blog. Blog is short for "web log" and it's effectively an online journal. Each entry that you write in your blog is known as a "post". In your blog you can post about anything you like, but obviously it's best if it relates in some way to your book. Here are some possible reasons to blog:

- To share with your readers some interesting research behind your book.

- To review a book in the same genre as yours (in this case, try to get reciprocal links between your site and that author's website).

- To give an account of progress in writing your next book.

- To report on an item in the national news that has some connection with your book.

- To provide feedback on a public event you've just held, such as a reading or book signing.

You can blog as often as you like, on anything you like that is associated with your book and your work, but be warned – it's addictive! It's also excellent practice in keeping up your writing habits and honing a short piece of prose.

Robert O Russell, for example, who recently published the first in a planned series of Christian books, under the brand Belief Books, is using his blog effectively to build an audience for the series, and posts regular poems tagged with appropriate words to appeal to people of his faith. It complements his book series and also keeps his hand in, between projects. You can view his website at www.belief-books.com.

Whatever the topic of your book, there's bound to be at least one blogger out there who shares your passion. Even the most obscure title will find its match in some quarter. I was once trying to find a special interest group for Pip Westgate's children's novel about a group of native Canadians that I'd never heard of, couldn't spell and couldn't pronounce: the Gitxsan tribe. The first internet search I did introduced me to www.gitxsan.com – surely a well-matched target audience if ever there was one!

Your blog doesn't even have to be in prose. If you're a poet, try posting a daily or weekly poem, suitably tagged. Internet users from all over the world who search for "poems about Christmas" or "funny poetry" will soon discover your work in this way and, once they've found and enjoyed one poem, they will be tempted to come back for more – and they may even order a copy of your book. Result!

It's worth mentioning here that if you run an interesting blog, regularly updated, you may attract subscribers. These are people who sign up to be sent, free of charge, an email of every new blog post that you write. This is an excellent low-cost way of building up a loyal fan base: all you have to input is your time. You should invite all your personal contacts to be subscribers too. This extra readership will help boost your ranking before those all-powerful search engines.

If you wish to, you can allow your website viewers to comment on your blog posts or other pages by filling in a comment form. This is a great way of getting feedback about your book and also about your website. (One of the joys of websites, unlike printed books, is that you can keep editing and changing them *ad infinitum*, so if you get a good suggestion from a viewer, you can implement it at no extra cost.) It's advisable to make sure that you have the chance to see and approve any comments before they appear on your website, and this is generally easy to set up. You can choose to be sent an email alert every time a comment is submitted, and then you can review it and approve it (or not) without delay.

Getting comments from readers is a really great feeling – but beware, there are unscrupulous spammers out there. These may post what at first seems like gushing praise of your website, but they'll include a link back to their own, usually a hard sell for a dubious product. They hope that you'll be so pleased with their praise that you'll post their comment unchecked, straight on to your website, embedding the link to their sales pitch to reach your readers too – a real cuckoo in the nest.

These scams can be callous and cruel. After writing in my personal blog about my daughter's Type 1 diabetes, I had several messages full of praise from companies with the give-away words "diabetes marketing" in their email address. They were hoping to sell me quack remedies. There IS no cure for Type 1 diabetes (though I'm hopeful that one day there will be, through the pioneering work of the Juvenile Diabetes Research Foundation).

If the wording of a comment sounds foreign or ungrammatical, doesn't specifically relate to your content, and is full of unmitigated praise, it's almost certainly spam. A light-hearted blog post I wrote about teaching my daughter to blow bubblegum bubbles yielded the comment:

> Admiring the hard work you put into your blog and detailed information you offer. It's nice to come across a website once in a while that isn't the same unwanted rehashed material. Wonderful read! I've saved your site and I'm adding your RSS feeds to my Google account.

It came from an email address to do with "Career Development Loans". Presumably they thought I had more potential than blowing bubbles! That one went straight into my trash box. I've come across many blogs which have proudly but unthinkingly published reams of such comments, which undermine the author's credibility and that's a real shame.

Following Others' Blogs

This brings me neatly on to the subject of following other authors' blogs. This is a great way to raise your profile and your own page views. Google other authors and books who are writing in the same field as you. Comment on their blogs. Review their books. Most of them will click on your signature to see who you are, and voilà, you get a hit back! Make sure you always use a signature that provides a link back through to your blog so they can do this. There is a real camaraderie among bloggers and it tends to be a very supportive network – although sadly there are cyber-bullies who post mean comments too. That's another reason to make sure you approve comments before they appear on your site.

You can search online for the blogs of avid readers of your genre and offer to send them a free copy of your book for them to review online. There are many specific booklovers' blogs, revolving around reviews. Any matching your genre are worth approaching, but don't take offence if a blogger declines the opportunity. They can only read so many books and they're becoming overburdened. If you're lucky, this strategy can be developed into a "virtual book tour", introducing your work to a wider audience.

It's not just book blogs that are worth tracking down, but any blogs and websites relating to your special subject. From ecology to engineering, from zodiac signs to zumba – there are sure to be openings out there, just waiting for you to seize them.

I once wrote a personal blog post inspired by a visit to a tiny museum in Scotland and sent them the link out of courtesy. A few days later, I was wondering why my site was getting so many hits. It turned out the museum had posted a link to my blog on the museum's Facebook page with a glowing recommendation and many friends of the museum were checking it out!

It's also worth offering to write guest posts on other relevant blogs. These can be a great introduction to new readers, endorsed by the blog owner's tacit approval of your book. Don't forget to return the favour by highlighting these guest posts on your own website so that your fan base will visit your kind host.

Visitor Statistics

Checking out the number of visits made to your site can be cheering and compulsive, but don't get too carried away with your site traffic stats. Before you know it, you'll be spending more and more time reading other people's blogs, giving and receiving blog awards, exchanging wisecracks and losing sight of your blog's main purpose: to increase book sales. Better to have relatively low viewing figures from serious, worthwhile readers who buy your books than to have high hit rates artificially inflated by playing blog tag with other bloggers.

To help you work out the quality of your hits, use a service such as Google Analytics to profile who is viewing your site. Your hits can be broken down by factors such as country, search engine, referrer, dwell-time (how long people spend on your site on average) and bounce rate (i.e. how many visitors leave your site immediately they arrive because it's not what they were really looking for). You can also discover which are the most and least popular pages. Use this advice to improve your website's effectiveness: add more of what works, remove what doesn't. Always think quality, not quantity.

Other Online Author Profiles

As well as your attractive website and lively blog, there are many other places online to establish a profile as an author. Not only that, but you can use them to make friends, connect with readers and other writers and generally inhabit the online world of books.

Let's look at a few now:

Author Central

Amazon Author Central is a free showcase provided by one of the world's largest retailers for you as a writer to help you promote your book (after all, it's in Amazon's interest for your book to be successful and sell copies). Only you can access this area, so don't expect your publisher or even Amazon to update it for you. Search for your book using its ISBN and as soon as it shows up on Amazon, begin to enhance your Author Central page. Go to https://authorcentral.amazon.co.uk in the UK and https://authorcentral.amazon.com/ in the USA (at the time of writing, these weren't linked so authors have to update both sites). Prepare and add a short biography, because readers are almost always interested in knowing a little more about authors. If you're comfortable doing so, upload an author picture of you looking friendly and interesting because this looks so much better than the Amazon-generated grey silhouette. Make sure you've mentioned your website address or invited people to connect with you on Facebook, Twitter, LinkedIn or any social media that you're on. (More about these in a moment!)

Book Fan Sites

There are a profusion of sites where enthusiastic book fans gather (in a "virtual" sense) to share opinions about books and make recommendations. Popular and well-known sites like GoodReads, Shelfari and Library Thing are just the tip of the iceberg. As bookshops disappear from our high streets and broadsheet newspapers focus on books that are destined for bestseller status, many readers are turning to other trusted sources for their reading recommendations. Independent book review sites are increasingly becoming the place to go to find out what everyone's reading. Make sure you and your book are listed there, that your profile is up to date, that you join groups and interact with readers, and that you're generally "available". Keep an eye on how popular mainstream authors operate on these sites and aim to follow their lead! Don't neglect to post reviews and comments on other authors' books too. This will help raise your profile and attract new readers. Other authors read books too!

Facebook, Twitter and other Online Social Networks

Of course, the internet is not just about websites. Unless you're a time-traveller who's only just touched down in the twenty-first century, you will have heard of the huge phenomenon of online social networking. Very many sites exist that allow you to network online with family and friends that you already know and to gain more friends that you may never meet in real life. Facebook and Twitter are the most popular two at the time of writing. LinkedIn is their more serious business-like cousin, Pinterest is the new kid on the block and GoodReads is gaining ground with the bookish. If you're not already on any of these, it's worth joining at least some of them to gain further platforms on which to promote your book.

Social networks are great ways of raising your profile and usually (and seductively) completely free of charge to use. The service provider's profits come from the advertising they feature. After signing up and gaining a username and password, you are given an online identity and the opportunity to connect with like-minded people. You input your thoughts and comments into the system whenever you like, about whatever you like – from news of what you had for breakfast to your views on the latest world event. You choose who you want to see your status updates and depending on the degree of privacy you've chosen, your friends may pass on your comments to their friends, and so on. Think about the famous six degrees of separation: you might assume that if you spend enough time on social networking sites, you'll eventually have canvassed the whole world. (Well, it's an agreeable theory to believe!)

In this way, you can reasonably quickly gain introductions to a wide range of people all over the world. If you enjoy this, you can build up a good following – but as with blogging, it can become addictive, and before you know it, you're spending hours swapping wisecracks with people on the other side of the world and neglecting to speak to your family in the same room as you. Just don't get me started on Twitter's #hashtag game, or I'll never finish writing this book…

Friends Forever?
Facebook and Twitter are the two most popular social networks at the time of writing, but this could easily change. Not long ago MySpace and Bebo were all the rage, and Friends Reunited was a big player, but these have now all but disappeared. This is a salutary lesson in why you shouldn't put all your promotional eggs in one basket in case that basket disappears.

That's also a reason why many authors are now choosing to assemble private mailing lists of their readers and online correspondents, so that they may target them directly with e-newsletters. This is, in any case, a useful tactic, as it allows you to take centre-stage and talk directly to them in any format you choose, without the constraints of social network sites. To start your own e-newsletter mailing list, add a response form to your website, inviting people to sign up for it. Send out your newsletter often enough to gain familiarity but not so often as to become tiresome – I'd suggest no more than once a month. Once a quarter would be ideal. Include only concise, interesting and well-presented news, including some special items only available to these subscribers – that will make them value it more. You might like to subscribe to a specialist service such as MailChimp, or stick to your usual email provider. David Ebsworth's newsletter is a great example of a simple, newsy, friendly and welcome bulletin – see www.davidebsworth.com for details. Whatever you do, ensure you don't include your mailing list with every email (enter the addresses in the "bcc" field, rather than the "to" field of your "compose email" template). Remember to send it only to those who have specifically consented and if they ask to be unsubscribed, do so promptly. Otherwise you'll fall foul of the Data Protection Act. But we digress from social media…

The Difference Between Facebook and Twitter

How much you benefit from Facebook and Twitter depends on how you use them. Many people say "I'm on Facebook, so I'm not bothering with Twitter", but they are not equivalent or interchangeable. I would define the chief difference between them is that Facebook is more personal and intimate and therefore the one to use to engage with existing friends and family, wherever they are in the world. Twitter, which allows you more privacy, enables you to reach out to people that you don't know. On Facebook, discussions are between you and your established "Facebook friends". On Twitter, conversations are tied together by hashtags i.e.words prefixed with # such as #books. People search against the hashtags that interest them and get involved in conversations this way, rather than seeking out individuals with which to engage. This means that if you can identify hashtags appropriate to your book you can easily seek out people on Twitter who share that interest, even if you know nothing else about them. To find possible new readers for his Star Trek inspired sci-fi novel, Adongiva, Jim Costello might seek out "#startrek", "#scifi" or even "#klingon"!

Another important difference is space. Facebook allows you to set up extensive descriptions about yourself, your background, your interests and your hobbies. You can store large galleries of photographs. You can also set up pages devoted to a subject or to manage an event, issuing invitations and receiving RSVPs. (It's great for publicising a book launch.)

Twitter prides itself on its economy of space: just 160 characters for your profile, and even that is luxury compared to the 140 character limit for your status updates known on Twitter as "tweets". You might be amazed to discover how effectively key ideas can be communicated within such concise limits. (That last sentence was 104 characters, by the way.) You'll also be pleasantly surprised at how easy it is to compose powerful tweets that include a couple of hashtags plus a link to the relevant part of your website – which of course is where you should be trying to drive potential purchasers.

Whatever you do, *don't* use Facebook, Twitter or any other social media simply to post up a string of free adverts about your book. If you do, people will ignore you. The trick is to involve individuals in interesting discussions and to build a reputation as a person worth engaging with. Their interest in buying your book will follow naturally.

It *is* acceptable etiquette to announce special offers on your books, just occasionally, as a favour to your followers. If they like you and enjoy your company, they'll be likely to post good reviews and tell their friends about your book. Do it too often and you'll devalue your currency. Some book promotion specialists say the ratio of interesting content to book-related information should be ninety-five to five.

If all this still sounds a bit complicated, don't be deterred. Many authors swear by the power of social networks to connect them with potential book-buyers and their established readers too. They're also a great way to befriend other authors and to share helpful advice. Never underestimate their power. Don't forget, these days strategic use of Twitter can overthrow a government!

To start using Facebook, go to www.facebook.com, click "Sign up" and follow the instructions. To start using Twitter, do the same at www.twitter.com. There are abundant tutorials and help sections on both. Further reading is also available. As a starting point try *Tweet Right* by Nicola Morgan, available as an e-book from Amazon. (If you don't have an e-reader, go to www.amazon.co.uk and download their free Kindle app to your computer or smartphone.)

Still not convinced? Well, take heart, because these online offerings are not the only social networks. There are still the old-fashioned types at which you can meet real people in the flesh. Let's take a look at these next.

7

A Network by Any Other Name

Exploiting Other Networks

What's in a name? That which we call a rose
By any other name would smell as sweet.
Juliet, in *Romeo & Juliet* by William Shakespeare

Of course, the internet is not the only network available to you. There are lots of other places where you can promote your book. If you think about it, you'll probably find you're already a member of quite a few. There are plenty more awaiting your arrival, giving you the opportunity to raise the profile of your book before a wider audience.

Use the following list as a starting point to research other potential platforms to promote your book.

Local Book Fairs

There seem to be ever more local book fairs around the country, either run by dedicated organising bodies, such as the Cheltenham Festival Office and Hay-on-Wye or by individual independent bookshops. Close to where I live in the Cotswolds, The Yellow-Lighted Bookshop, with branches in Tetbury and Nailsworth, recently pulled off an audacious launch of its own book festival, smack between two long-established literary fairs in Cheltenham and Bath. The national appetite to attend author talks shows no sign of abating. If you are lucky enough to have a book fair near you, speak to the event organiser well in advance and you may be able to stage an author event of your own. While major events with a national profile will be completely booked up with bestselling celebrity authors, backed by publishers' marketing budgets, it is always worth asking. If you're feeling brave, try rallying other local self-published authors to launch your own "fringe" event!

Custom-made Special Events

A group of Bristol-based writers sharing pirates as their theme cleverly devised, to great effect, a public theme day called "Bristol's Big Pirate Party", full of photo opportunities. Well promoted in advance, this high profile event was a great platform for the promotion of *The Black Banner*, a new children's novel by Helen Hart, ("Treasure Island for girls", as one reviewer put it), the recently reissued work of historical novelist Helen Hollick and a book from the Long John Silver Trust lobbying for a Treasure Island tourist trail in this ancient seafaring city. To cap it all, the Bristol Old Vic Theatre got involved to publicise their own outdoor summer run of Robert Louis Stevenson's *Treasure Island*. The city of Bristol embraced the occasion, with hundreds of people turning up on the harbourside in full pirate costume to welcome the replica ship *The Matthew* as it arrived at the docks, cannons blazing. BBC Radio presenter Steve Yabbsley judged a children's pirate fancy dress competition and broadcast live from the event.

Could you manage something similar in your area?

Library Events

Libraries are always keen to host events that will encourage local people to visit them, so it is worth talking to your library manager to see if you can engineer a "meet the author" afternoon or evening to share your experience of self-publishing with library members. You may sell only a handful of copies of your book at the event, but the advance publicity promoting the event in the library and by word-of-mouth afterwards will, in itself, raise awareness and interest. You can also present your event as a news story, before and afterwards, to your local papers. These occasions are particularly welcome if you're a children's author and can offer a fun event at half-term or during the holidays. Don't expect to be paid for your time, but you can easily and cheaply maximise the publicity with giveaways such as bookmarks and colouring sheets. All of which mention your book and your website URL, of course!

Book Groups

An abundance of book groups meet regularly in various locations, sometimes linked to libraries, bookshops and local interest groups. These generally operate by choosing a book to read each month for discussion at the following meeting. You could offer to come along as a visiting author offering to sell copies of your book at a reduced rate (potentially a great local paper story too).

Even if they don't have their own book group, social clubs such as WIs often invite a different local speaker to every meeting, and you could offer your services to talk about your book and the self-publishing process – or about the subject matter of your book, if that's more appropriate.

Writers Circles

Throughout the country, many writers' circles bring together aspiring authors and poets to give each other moral support, share their experience and critique each other's work. If you're not already a member of the ones closest to your home, search them out and offer to visit. After talking about your publishing experiences, you may not only sell some copies of your book but also have the chance to make supportive friends who will help you promote your work and encourage you in future writing projects.

Special Interest Exhibitions and Rallies

Motor sports events have been very useful for author Nigel S Dobbie to promote his highly acclaimed book about Corvette racing. These are attended by people who are huge enthusiasts for this particular form of motor racing and many are prepared to pay the cover price of £60 per copy for his beautifully produced, comprehensive guide. There might be a similar meeting relevant to your book.

Schools and Other Educational Institutes

Most schools are involved with at least one national literacy event each school year, such as World Book Day (usually held in early March, targeting schoolchildren of all ages) and National Children's Book Week (in the autumn term and aimed at primary schools). Particularly during these events, but also during the rest of the year, many schools welcome visiting authors to talk to the children about what it's like to write a book. If you are a children's author, you could give readings of your book or run a workshop for children to write their own story. You could even run a competition, with the child who writes the best story being given a free signed copy of your book. Your visit might also lend itself to themed activity for the day, such as dressing to match the period in which your book is set. If you have children of your own, or some other connection with a suitable school, don't hesitate to use them as a testing ground.

- Tanya Maude, author of *Monty Banana and the Roller Skates*, found her children's school very receptive to a puppet show project that takes the book as its theme.

- Author Richard Denning, who writes historical, time-travel fantasy stories, has cleverly engineered his busy school visit programme to match different aspects of the curriculum, from English and literacy to history and the physics of time-travel.

- Helen Hart, author of *The Black Banner*, a children's novel about a girl pirate, visits schools in her pirate outfit – a great ice-breaker – to engage them with her book.

Some schools set aside a budget for this activity, so sound them out to see if they'll pay a fee or at least your travelling expenses. Those strapped for cash will welcome the offer of a free visit. Contact the headteacher in small schools, the teacher in charge of Literacy for larger primary schools, and the Head of English for secondary schools, unless you are proposing a talk that relates to a different subject in the curriculum. Suggest you bring copies of your book to sign and sell for those who want to buy one. Bear in mind that children will need advance warning to bring in money and that your price will need to be affordable on a pocket-money budget. A special discount for the day will be much appreciated.

School visits are also great opportunities to promote your book in the local papers and to gain valuable photographs of eager young readers enjoying your book – great collateral for your website where they will help clinch sales. There's a good example at www.janchez.com, the website of writer and illustrator Janet Szczesniak, author of *The Frog Who Made Friends*. Remember that schools must have written permission from a parent or guardian for a child to be photographed, so only take pictures with the school's cooperation and make sure they have received the necessary consent. (This isn't as tricky as it sounds – most schools get a single waiver form signed for each child at the start of the year.)

Secondary schools may also be interested in career-oriented talks about being an author. Approach the Head of Careers if you'd like to help in this way.

Other Local Groups

Depending on the nature of your book, there may also be other local groups that you could target. A novel for young adults could be of interest to your local youth club; a non-fiction book about local history would appeal to a local history society.

With all of these networking activities, it's up to you to decide how far afield you want to go. If you're prepared to cover the travel costs – or if the group you are visiting is willing to pay them – you can probably drum up quite a lot of events of this nature, all of which will provide valuable PR opportunities in the areas that you visit. If you live in London but do a talk at a Brighton school, the Brighton press (not normally interested in you as a Londoner) may still be persuaded to run a story because the school you're visiting is in their catchment area. Talks provide the ideal opportunity to put out your feelers beyond your usual territory.

If you have a good experience with any of these groups, encourage them to pass your details on to their own contacts. The headteacher of a school that you charm could be easily persuaded to promote your services to other schools in his or her local education authority. WI groups can recommend you to other branches in their nationwide network. Before you know it, you could have quite a few bookings and be introduced to hundreds of potential new readers.

All of these opportunities can rack up a lot of time, trouble and travel costs. Even if you really enjoy them, decide early on just how much of each you prepared to invest. We'll cover budget later, in Chapter 11. In the meantime, let's pay a visit to the more traditional means of selling books: the bookshop.

8

Shop!

Getting the Retailer's Attention

Customer: My children are climbing your bookshelves. That's OK,
isn't it? They won't topple over, will they?
Jen Campbell, in *Weird Things People Say In Bookshops*

Unless you are planning to sell all your books individually to personal contacts, you will want high street retailers to sell them on your behalf. Having your book stocked in shops enhances your credibility as a serious author, and also offers you venues for signings and other author events. However, these days the author must consider not just the physical shops on the high street, but also the substantial and growing online marketplaces – especially if you've opted for an e-book edition of your book.

I'm using the term "high street" pretty loosely here. Major bookstores will be well represented in out-of-town malls, retail parks and "shopping villages". There are other kinds of retailers that may stock a few books relevant to their main line of business, such as local history books in museums. What all of these outlets have in common is that they provide a local platform where the potential buyer can actually see your book, pick it up, flick through it and read a bit before making the decision to buy. It is still much more tactile than the online shopping experience. High street shops also offer the presence of an expert to guide readers' buying decisions: the shop assistant.

Online retailers might protest at this point. They do,

after all, feature numerous online reviews, high-technological means to "see inside this book!" and free e-book sampling. Nonetheless, buying a book in a store bookshop remains a much more interactive and personal experience than shopping online. You also have a much greater chance of building a personal relationship with your local bookshop manager than you do with a giant such as Amazon.

Although both traditional shops and online retailers provide the same function for you – supplying copies of your book to readers in exchange for payment – they operate very differently.

Let's consider high street retailers first.

High Street Retailers
High street retailers who sell books may be:

- Independent retailers who specialise in books.

- Independent traders who sell books as part of a wider range of products.

- Major retail chains of bookstores, such as Waterstones.

- Major retailers such as supermarkets and superstores who also sell books as a customer service.

First of all, be realistic and disregard your local supermarkets and superstores. They will have strict rules on their stocklines and merchandising. These are determined at corporate level rather than by your local store manager, although there is significant variation in the stock held in any supermarket which will match its range to the socio-economic profile of their catchment area. Visit two branches of the same chain, one in an affluent area and another in a deprived town, and you'll be able to spot it for yourself. These constraints will almost certainly preclude your book's chances of being stocked. Comfort yourself with the knowledge that they would offer you the least return per sale, and focus instead on the outlets more likely to stock your book at a more palatable discount. Let's give priority to the *most* likely outlet first: the independent local bookshop.

Independent Bookshops

If you have an independent bookseller operating nearby, you are very fortunate. A local bookshop may provide a more sympathetic reception than the big chains, so head there first. Not that the independent bookseller has less need to make a profit than the chainstore. "I love my job and I love books, but at the end of the day I have my mortgage to pay," says Hereward Corbett, proprietor of the highly regarded Yellow-Lighted Bookshop.

You may have dreamed of seeing your book in their window while you were writing it. However tempting it may be, do not rush to your local shop with a copy of your freshly-printed book and tackle them straight away. To stand the best chance of being stocked by high street bookshops at all, never mind getting pride of place, take a step back from your position as an author. Consider instead the retailer's point of view. Understand how you, as a local independently-published author, fit into the jigsaw of their business and you'll be more likely to be able to make a realistic proposition to the manager, who will be more likely to accept it.

Consider the Retailer's Viewpoint

All high street bookshops are under immense pressure to deliver profits in an increasingly difficult marketplace. Not only is their traditional monopoly on books being eroded by the growth of online retailers, but they are finding themselves undercut by three significant phenomena within the high street itself:

- Supermarkets cherry-picking bestsellers, offering an extremely limited range of books at heavily discounted prices.

- Remainder bookstores appealing to book-buyers on a low budget, stocking relatively new titles in perfect condition, sourced from returns of unsold copies from mainstream book retailers to distributors.

- Charity bookshops offering a vast range of books for all ages at tiny prices, made possible by their low running costs (exempt from business rates, stock that costs nothing to acquire, and volunteer staff that work for free).

In times of recession, the purchase of a new book from a bookshop for oneself can feel like a reckless extravagance. People are looking for bargains. Frighteningly, there are now more "pound shops" (where every item costs £1) than bookshops on British high streets. It's no wonder that bookshop managers are feeling anxious and risk-averse. Bear in mind this precarious operating environment when you make your first approach to your local bookstore.

Another important consideration is the way in which high street bookstores buy their stock. They are not used to authors turning up in person to make a sales pitch for their book. Yes, they receive representation – but from publishers' professional salesmen who promote dozens of books at a time in a swift and clinical way. When I visited Hereward Corbett in his Tetbury shop, he had just finished a meeting with a rep from a major mainstream publisher. "He gave their 100 latest books a pitch of just ten seconds each," he told me.

A single visit from the publisher's sales representative thus enabled the bookseller to acquaint himself quickly and easily with a large number of genres, books and authors in a very short space of time, freeing him up to concentrate on the running of his shop (and to chat to me, the customer).

"Publishers effectively act as filters for retailers," explains Hereward, who had a long career with major book retail chains before launching his own independent bookshops. "Publishers are the bookseller's quality control mechanism and we trust their judgement."

By buying primarily from publishers, retailers are guaranteed a stock of commercially viable books. They benefit from a discount of thirty to forty per cent, thirty day credit terms and consolidated, single invoices for large quantities of books. This streamlines their accounting operations and benefits their cash-flow.

Sales reps' visits are part of the mainstream publishers' large publicity machine, which also includes advertising, media presence, and author events. The actual delivery of books to bookshops is done by distributors – chiefly by two large organisations, Bertrams and Gardners. The publishers provide vast stocks of their books to these distributors, who then run a slick service to retail outlets.

Distributors offer just-in-time delivery, which means that books sold one day can be replenished the next. The bookseller thus maintains very low stock levels of each book – typically just two or three copies – which enables him to carry a broader range of titles and to please more customers. There's also a guarantee of sale-or-return, so the retailer takes no risk by stocking a title – it's simply a question of making judicial use of his shelf space and matching the range of books to his local clientele's needs. Booksellers receive next-day delivery on most books ordered in response to customers' particular requests.

"Amazon has been very clever in suggesting to the public that there is something special about their next-day delivery service, for which you generally have to pay a premium," advises Hereward. "But actually, your local bookshop is able to offer the same next-day ordering facility at no extra cost to you, the customer."

Now consider how it must seem to a bookstore manager when approached by you as a self-published author keen to have his books stocked:

- You are not a slick sales rep practised at making a speedy pitch.

- Your book has not passed the quality test demanded by mainstream publishers.

- You have no guaranteed next-day delivery service.

- You do not have an agreed discount scheme in place.

- You do not have the publicity machine of a large publisher behind you.

But you *do* have several important assets that no publisher's rep can compete with:

- You are a local resident with a circle of local friends and relations who are soft targets for your book.

- You have a passion about your book and a special focus on your subject.

- You have unrivalled specialist knowledge of your book. Indeed, there are probably large chunks of it that you can recite!

Therefore when you go to the bookshop to make your pitch, play to your strengths, while demonstrating your understanding and sympathy for the bookseller's lot.

So here is a guide to planning your pitch to your local bookshop:

Firstly, do some research. If you're not already a regular customer of the shop, visit several times before you make your sales approach. Get to know how it operates and who it serves. Buy books and chat pleasantly to the staff as you make your purchase. If you charm them, they may be especially sympathetic when you return to make your pitch. Equally, if you alienate them with unreasonable demands or by showing airs and graces, they may remember you for all the wrong reasons and actively resist promoting your book when the time comes.

Check out not just the staff, but the customers also. Spy on the clientele to identify what kind of people favour this particular shop. It will vary according to the time of day – office workers at lunchtime, families after school, etc. Notice whether the shop runs any customer events such as book signings, book launches or book groups. If it does, go along as a fly-on-the-wall – see how they operate, whether they're successful, and decide whether you could offer and benefit from something similar.

If any other local authors are being promoted within the shop, track them down and befriend them. Find out the secrets of their success – and be prepared to share your experiences with them too. You may even decide to join forces to present themed promotions for local writers (more on special events in Chapter 9).

Do all of this in small bursts, buying books along the way – you don't want to be mistaken, lingering in the shadows, for a shoplifter!

Find out whether the shop has a website specifically for its branch – and if so, explore it. If it has a Facebook page, "like" it and become a Facebook friend. If it is on Twitter, "follow" it, and re-tweet any appropriate tweets to your followers. You should soon get to know the shop and its customer profile well.

Then arrange a specific appointment to meet the manager at a time when you expect the shop to be quiet. Ask advice from counter staff as to the best time to do this – for example, a day when he won't be preoccupied with incoming deliveries or visits from publishers' reps. Don't make it close to his lunch break or closing time when he'll be pressed for time and making surreptitious glances at his watch. Make an appointment for a specific time to make your case formally.

Turn up on time, in the right place, dressed in a presentable manner suitable for your book and genre. This isn't a job interview – the typical sales rep's business suit is unlikely to be right unless your book is aimed at the business sector – but you do need to be business-like in your thinking.

Take with you some carefully prepared ammunition, including several copies of your book. If you convince the manager to stock it, you will then be able to take him up on the deal straight away! But books alone are not enough...

If you have local press cuttings, (see Chapter 10 for how to get some) take copies that you can leave with him for display or simply for consideration. "As seen in" signs are always influential. If you haven't yet achieved any press coverage but know you will do soon, update him with anticipated publication dates of such items. Make sure they are presented to the best advantage – photocopied or scanned clearly (in colour if the original was in colour), aligned straight with the page, neatly trimmed and annotated with the title and date of the publication in which they appeared.

If you have been on local radio talking about your book, provide a note of the station, programme, interviewer and the time and date of the broadcast; if you have a transcript, even better. The manager is unlikely to read it at your meeting, but it adds credibility to your pitch as a professional author.

Provide a clear note of your book's price and the discount you are willing to offer, print a professional-looking "bookseller information sheet" on headed notepaper giving full contact details – your address, landline, mobile, email, website address, Facebook page name, Twitter account. You might also take print-outs of relevant pages from your website to explain your background and how you came to write this book.

If you have invested in promotional materials, such as postcards or bookmarks (see Chapter 9), take a good supply of these too. A colourful card in an eye-catching colour and design to attach to the book's cover proclaiming "local author" might also be appreciated.

Present all of these things neatly in a slim folder that you can leave behind with your contact and you'll also leave a strong first impression as a professional, business-minded marketer that will be a positive asset to the bookshop's profitability.

And now is your moment! Outline your book as a business proposition, and make a case for the bookstore to dedicate a bit of shelf space in return for a good profit on every copy sold.

Make a clear offer of discounts, sale-or-return deadlines and delivery promises, couched in terms that will appeal to the trader. Demonstrate the local following that you have already established. Make it clear you have fuelled a local demand which needs to be met somewhere – and make it clear you'd rather it was in his shop by offering to advertise his bookshop on your website.

If you belong to a local writers group or other special interest group relating to your book, mention this. Offer to drive these people in to his shop and then follow through by sending a few of them in. I've heard of one self-published author who primed friends to go in to local bookstores asking if they stocked his book and feigning disappointment when they didn't. The author hoped to have demonstrated local demand and encourage a reluctant trader to be more receptive. You may not feel comfortable resorting to this slightly underhand method, but it worked for him!

If the store manager is receptive and agrees to stock your book, thank him heartily and be sure to keep any promises you have made. Honour your side of the bargain and he'll be more likely to do long-term trade with you.

Now would also be a good time to discuss opportunities for in-store events to fuel sales of your book. Many store managers will welcome such events, not only to sell copies of the book promoted, but because they pull more customers into the shop to buy other things. (See Chapter 9 for event recommendations.)

Once you've secured your stock provision, don't consider your task complete. To keep that particular plate spinning while you tackle other promotional opportunities, you should revisit regularly, but not with a frequency that could be taken for obsession or lack of anything better to do. Keep the manager and staff posted with progress that might encourage them to promote your book, such as new press cuttings and radio airtime, or favourable reviews from significant sources. After all, every little helps. (I *so* wish that wasn't a supermarket slogan!)

Bookshop Chains

Getting your book accepted by one or more independent local bookshops should make you feel confident enough to tackle local branches of major bookshop chains. As mentioned earlier, although there will be a locally-based manager, stocks and policies will be dictated from regional or national headquarters and the store will also be under orders to deliver specific profits. Even so, the manager will have some flexibility to entertain propositions from local authors. Many authors have found the local branch of a major bookstore to be extremely supportive.

Although you're more likely to find a large-scale promotion for a particular book in chainstores than in independent shops, don't allow these to generate false hope for your own book. It's not there just because the manager is exceptionally fond of this book, but because the promotional scheme is a nice little earner, supplementing book sales.

"Any book you see prominently displayed in these shops has had its space in the shop bought and paid for by the publishers," advises Amelia Fairney, Publicity Director at Penguin Books (General).

In any case, such a display is not an author's right – and if you ask for similar treatment, you will get short shrift.

Just as in the independent bookstores, your best chance of getting your book stocked is to convince the manager that any shelf space given to your book will be as profitable as that given to those from mainstream publishers. Take the same approach as you did for the independents, but make more allowances for the constraints from head office.

Pick Your Territory

Try to get your book stocked in all the high street bookshops local to you. Operate within the radius in which you are prepared to travel and in which your book will be accepted as a local product.

This isn't necessarily a simple task of drawing a circle with a 20-mile radius from your house. There are odd pre-conceptions in this country of what exactly is local. In a built-up area with a dense population, local may mean a radius of just three miles, but it may cover more people than a 20-mile radius in more rural areas.

There are fierce local loyalties to contend with. Two independent bookshops may be just a few miles apart geographically, but if they belong to different counties or even countries, their stock may be very different. A book about English legends may be well received in Gloucester, but drop over the border into Gwent and it may be perceived as alien. Even within England, rivalries exist between adjacent counties such as Lancashire and Yorkshire or Gloucestershire and Wiltshire. These may preclude your book from being stocked by a shop that is geographically closer to your home.

The two branches of Hereward Corbett's Yellow-Lighted Bookshop are only five miles apart in Cotswold market towns, but their clientele is quite different. Tetbury is very much on the tourist route for its proximity to two major tourist attractions: the National Arboretum at Westonbirt and the Prince of Wales' country residence, Highgrove. It is also at the heartland of the Beaufort Hunt country. Its stock is chosen to appeal to these specific interests. The bookshop's Top Ten listing bears little relation to national lists, *The Little Book of Hunting* being a particular recent bestseller in Tetbury.

By contrast, the Nailsworth shop is more about engaging with local residents than with tourists. Be on the lookout for such variances – and opportunities – as you research your local bookstores. Also be aware that your subject matter might appeal to local bookstores outside of your own home territory. Jill Rutherford's memoir of her days in Japan would surely sell as well in any English language bookstore in that country as in her adoptive home of Eastbourne.

Special Interest Shops

Of course, local bookstores are not the only independent shops that might sell your books. Other kinds of retailers such as tourist information offices, tea shops, museums and gift shops may all sell locally sourced books as souvenirs. Professor William Fairney's tongue-in-cheek but technically sound guide *How to Build a Lead Balloon* makes a fun and affordable souvenir in local science and design museums. Jane Dismore's biography of Pamela Hambro, *A Voice from the Garden*, would be an asset to the gift shops of any of the stately homes that feature in its pages. Think laterally if you are to saturate all your potential book traders, near and far.

If you want to gain a presence in bookshops where you can't play the local card, your best advice is make sure your book has an ISBN and is registered with Nielsen BookData (www.nielsenbookdata.co.uk). Also list your book with major wholesalers such as Gardners Books (www.gardners.com) and Bertrams (www.bertrams.com). Do plenty of promotion, including calling bookshops yourself, and make sure the book shows as available on online catalogues. That way, stock can be pulled through by individual stores as your promotional campaign takes hold, and as local satisfied readers spread the word further afield.

Distribution

Some retailers may ask you who your distributor is. This is because mainstream publishers tend to use distributors as an efficient and trusted way of getting their book from point A to point B. However, using a distributor can be costly, as many will request a trade discount of at least sixty per cent, plus a decent level of stock (200 copies – a tall order when your print run is probably little more than that). Also, distributors are naturally nervous about taking on an unproved self-published title that may not sell well.

For this reason, most self-publishers either handle their own distribution or it's handled by their publishing services company. Alternatively, they may have elected for Print on Demand, in which case distribution is likely to be handled by the Ingram Book Group, one of the world's largest book distribution companies.

Not having a third party distributor won't be a deal-breaker for most retailers. They just want to know that if they order the book, it's going to get to them quickly and efficiently, with a decent discount applied. So if you're handling distribution yourself, reassure them that your book is registered with Nielsen BookData, that you or your publishing services company receives tele-ordering and that orders will be despatched promptly with the right paperwork – normally an invoice with an order reference on it.

Do not despair if you fail to get your book stocked in any physical bookshops, because being on a bookshop shelf is less critical to your book's success than it used to be. Online sales are far more important, accounting for nearly ninety per cent of all book sales according to one mainstream publisher. So, it's to online stores that we turn next.

Online Book Retailers

Compared to high street retailers, online bookstores seem intangible. They may promise greater sales, but you can't have the comfort of a cosy chat with the staff about your book. Not surprisingly, these sellers must be tackled in an entirely different way.

Many view Amazon like some little-known, much-feared mythical beast. There are various theories about the way they choose what to highlight. There is no definitive guide to follow, but there are some common sense rules.

First, you need to realise that as soon as your book is published, it will, as if by magic, be listed by Amazon (and other online book retailers). At Amazon, they suck in basic book data supplied by Nielsen BookData, via the central directory of ISBN numbers – the title, author, publication date, dimensions, number of pages, format. If someone searches online for your title, Amazon will display a page about your book based on this data. It may indicate an "out of stock" status initially, but if someone is prepared to pay for your book Amazon will order and deliver it.

Not every purchaser goes to the Amazon website to look only for a specific title. Even if they do, they don't always buy what they were originally seeking. They may instead purchase alternatives suggested by its search engine. If you've ever looked for a book on Amazon, you'll probably have noticed two sections beneath the details of that book, headed "Frequently bought together" and "Customers who bought this item also bought..."

This is the virtual shelf effect: Amazon is trying to show you the books that might sit next to your chosen book in a real bookshop. It may list different editions of the same book, such as hardback or paperback options, new and used, and it may show other books in the same genre. The results are sometimes surprising, because shoppers don't always buy books in the same genre in any particular transaction. I was searching for "books about Japan" recently (a little light industrial espionage for competitors to Jill Rutherford's book), and to my astonishment, up popped Jackie French's wonderful children's picture book, *Diary of a Wombat*. I'm very familiar with this book, as it's one of my small daughter's favourites. It has nothing to do with Japan, but Amazon put them together because they've recently had a shopper who just happened to buy both (as well as an Australian hat with corks, presumably to get the reader in the mood for the wombat's adventures).

These titles are being "pushed" to shoppers rather than "pulled" by them. You can increase your chances of having your book exposed in this way if you take a couple of constructive steps.

First, adjust the tags that have been applied to your book. Tags are similar to keywords used in websites. They are markers to define the genre of a book. Anyone can apply any tag to any book listed within Amazon. Below the book description is an invitation to do just that and an explanation of how to do so quickly and simply. The tags that you input are visible to everyone. So, if your book has been under-tagged in the past and you can think of other tags against which people might search for it, add them now. This gives your book a greater chance of being seen in future searches against that tag.

Although your book may appear in tagged searches for all the right tags, it may still only appear a long way down Amazon's listing, and not be seen by people who don't have the time or patience to scroll through numerous pages. Its position in the list is partly determined by the user, who can dictate the order in which their search displays items, according to various criteria – popularity, publication date and price. Even so, in a very popular genre, the items thrown up by this search may run to tens of thousands.

So, how to get yours nearer to the top?

Exactly how Amazon's search engine works is not public knowledge – and I suspect, like Google, they'd like to keep it that way, to guard against it being manipulated – but there are certain precautions that seem to help. They don't take much time, money or effort, so if you are serious about leaving no stone unturned in your quest to sell your books, you'd best try them out.

Firstly, log in to Amazon's Author Central and make sure your author profile is complete (did you miss that? If so, see Chapter 6). Next, encourage your readers to post positive reviews of your book. Potential purchasers are much more likely to buy your book if they see a string of stars by the listing, especially if they've never heard of your book before coming across it in a tag search. They are also likely to be swayed by the content of these online reviews. I always read at least a few reviews of any book I'm dithering about buying on Amazon. To my mind, publishing an unlimited number of reviews is Amazon's chief virtue, and you should take full advantage of this facility.

You will probably need to badger your friends to do this, especially if they're not regular Amazon reviewers. Readers seem happy to email you their rave reviews but don't realise what a difference it could make to your sales if they also posted them on Amazon. Keep asking them to do so until they comply. It's not possible for you to input their review on their behalf, as you'd need to use a login and password other than your own. No doubt this is what some people do, but I don't want to recommend anything that is not entirely honourable! No matter how many great compliments you have in your post-bag or on your website, you're missing a trick if they're not also on Amazon.

Don't be put off by the recent "sockpuppet" debate – posting genuine reviews is ethical, professional and common sense practice. But do take with a pinch of salt any books that boast exclusively five star (or indeed one star) ratings all written in the same style!

Rumour has it that once you've notched up a large number of reviews – possibly thirty-plus – the Amazon search engine will consider your book to be a potential top seller, and therefore start to list it much higher up its search pages.

Like all online services, its *modus operandi* can and will change frequently, so please do not take this as gospel – but given that it will cost you nothing but time to implement, it's well worth your best shot.

Unfortunately, not all great promotional activities are as cheap. In the next chapter, we'll consider how to make the most of whatever investment you can afford by way of promotional materials and events.

9

Pay Attention to Me!

Promotional Materials, Book Launches and Other Events

There is only one thing in the world worse than being talked about, and that is not being talked about.
Oscar Wilde, in *The Picture of Dorian Gray*

You will no doubt – and deservedly – have been very proud when you first held a printed copy of your book in your hands. You will have shown it to all and sundry – but although the book will take centre-stage in all of your promotional activities, it need not be your only prop. It's worth getting some other materials produced to help you draw attention to your book in a compact and cost-effective format, whether to provide a build-up to a book launch or simply to hand out to anyone you meet who you think may be interested in your book.

Promotional Materials

Any items you choose to produce should include:

- One or more striking images, including the cover of your book (so that it is easy to find a copy on the shelves).

- Your website URL (so that they can keep in touch with you and follow your blog).

- A photo of yourself – if you are willing – to raise your own profile (especially if the recipient doesn't already know you in person).

- Details of your publisher and any agreed stockists (likely to include at least your publisher's online bookshop).

Keep copies of these in your briefcase, wallet or handbag at all times, so that whenever you spot an opportunity to promote your book, you have them on hand.

These days, producing small quantities of promotional items is cheap and easy. In the old hot-metal and printing plate days, the set-up costs per page would have been huge, only defrayed by large print runs. You'd have been charged much the same price for 100 copies of an item as for 1,000. With digital printing, set-up costs are low, making modest print runs economically viable.

Give your publisher first refusal for printing your promotional materials. They will already have your book's artwork on file, including the cover image, and will be able to design materials to match your developing brand. Your website design should also be consistent with your chosen look. Then, if anyone sees any of these items in isolation, they will be able to tell at a glance that it relates to your book.

As a big buyer of print, your publisher should be able to negotiate good printing rates on your behalf. If they can't help, try local print shops on your high street. Outline your requirements and ask to see samples of similar jobs they've done for others. Get them to commit to a precise fixed quote and then repeat the process at others within your reach. You may be surprised at the variation in prices offered. If you try to save time by just visiting one print shop, you may well pay over the odds.

If you're comfortable with using the internet, check out some of the popular online design and print services. You may have come across these before. They often put flyers in parcels sent by other online suppliers. They keep their charges low by providing a choice of fixed design templates to which you add your own details. I've occasionally used services such as Vistaprint (www.vistaprint.com) and found them simple and competitively priced. But be warned, once you are enmeshed in these sites, they can become addictive! They will print everything imaginable, from postcards, posters and pens to t-shirts, car stickers and shopping bags, and they offer an online preview of how they'd look before you order. Of course, they look fabulous once you've added your particular book's image or title, and it's very easy to get carried away and spend more than you intended. Beware of handling charges, VAT and P&P, added at the checkout, which can double the price of the item. Handing out pens bearing your book's title may be fun but it's unlikely to boost your sales. However, used wisely, these services can be very handy indeed.

If you have a small supply of such materials to hand out, you'll be less likely to give away free copies of your book. There's no doubt that it does feel good to give a book away, especially one with an inscription, but do remember that unless you've published your book expressly to give away free of charge, your objective is to make sales. It's true that it makes sense to offer a certain number of free review copies, especially if you can do this in e-book format, but it's only worthwhile giving them to people who you are confident will read them and write a review (and put it on Amazon). You've laboured hard and invested substantially to get to this point, so make people pay for the privilege of owning a copy! Allocate a specific number of free review copies – say two to three per cent of your print run – and stick to it. The exception is if you have more than one e-book on offer, in which case one free e-book can be a useful loss-leader, triggering full price purchases of your other books.

Even media editors may not merit an unsolicited review copy. Bear in mind that these people may receive dozens of books every day from others in your position, but they can only read so many. Therefore precede your despatch of any review copies with a polite invitation. Only send an actual copy to those who personally accept. And even if they do accept, don't presume this will guarantee you a printed review. There again, if they can't be bothered to respond to your invitation, do you really think they are likely to read and review your book? Never follow up an unanswered invitation with a free book! (More on media relations in Chapter 10.)

Promotional Events

The most likely first event you will organise will be your book launch, but most of the advice below applies equally to any other kind of event.

Your book launch may be a private, invitation-only event to thank those who have supported you – friends, family, editors, publisher, etc. – or it might be thrown open to the wider world, to lure in potential purchasers and attract some media attention. Whatever you do is entirely up to you. Book launch parties are not compulsory and you can play them how you wish. Make the most of this unique opportunity to kick-start your book's sales by planning the whole event very carefully in advance. There are no absolute rules and every event will be different – and should be – just as every book is unique.

Here are some general guidelines to consider when you are planning your book launch:

Venue

Bookshops are the obvious place to hold launch events, as they exist to sell books, but they are not the only option. The manager may well be happy to organise this for you, especially if you persuade him that you will be inviting a lot of guests, all potential customers for his store. If you choose this route, take the manager's advice. He has a lot more experience of these events than you do and knows his clientele well.

It may be that the nature of your book suggests a specific venue relevant to its subject matter. Is there one that is more appropriate/practical/available/affordable for your launch? Hunt around, ask the advice of your local tourist office, and you may be surprised at the variety of low-cost options. (You'd need to sell an awful lot of books to justify a large venue hire charge.) If you can, identify a benefit for your chosen venue. If it's a pub, it will gain extra bar sales, or extra visitors if it's a museum. The venue's management might be glad of the extra publicity and media attention.

Your launch might have more impact and more appeal if you choose a venue that has a special significance for your book. Diesel Publishing launched Paul Hatch's *Evocative Tales*, a collection of myths about ancient Bristol, in an old boathouse on the harbourside, where one couldn't fail to be aware of this waterside city's historic past.

Alternatively you might find a venue with a steady traffic of people who might be interested in your subject matter, for example a tourist attraction or at a special event or trade fair. Paradoxically you may make more sales at a non-retail venue than in a bookshop.

Not all books will find such handy or appropriate venues for their launch and a bookstore launch can be very effective. Do not assume that just because it is a public place where people come to buy books, they will be interested in buying yours. Take responsibility for inviting some camp followers to avoid the embarrassment of sitting at a book signing table on your own. Try to bring along at least thirty friends and relations. If other shoppers see them queuing up at your signing table, they will pay more attention to you and your book and may even join the queue to buy a signed copy themselves! Here are some other useful pointers:

- Don't get stuck behind the signing table – go walkabout and chat with book browsers around the shop.

- Make the first move: introduce yourself to shoppers, especially those in your genre's area, with a charming, confident smile.

- Try "puppy-dog selling": put the book in the shopper's hands, because once they've handled it, they'll be more likely to buy.

- Match your sales pitch to each person, treat them like an individual and try to identify the "hot button" that will turn them on.

- When they're considering whether to buy it, offer to write a dedication on the first page – this one-off opportunity to make the book extra special for them might clinch the deal.

Timing

When planning your launch, consider which day of the week and what time of day will be most convenient for your typical buyer. It may not be the day or time that suits you best. For a children's book, it needs to be outside of the school day. It may be best at a weekend or in the school holidays when parents are actively seeking interesting, low-cost events to entertain their children. For a business book, early afternoon coincides with office workers' lunch breaks while an early evening slot might catch them on their way home.

Guest List

Do you want your launch to be open to anyone who's passing or should it be by invitation only? You probably have some people that you would like to thank for their support and who will want to help you celebrate. You may also think of some guests whose presence could persuade others to attend or attract press coverage, such as a local celebrity, mayor or MP.

Invitation Cards

Create the right mood and expectations by providing an attractive card that echoes the style and tone of your book. Produce it in both printed and email format. You can then use the email to invite a larger audience without increasing the cost, and as a reminder nearer the event date. Include an accurate map and postcode (for those finding it via satnav), a clear statement of the start time and of any timed events such as a speech, the details of your book including the cost (so they know how much money to bring to buy a copy!) and what kind of refreshments you will provide. If you'd like your guests to bring friends to swell the numbers, say so. Ask them to RSVP and provide an easy means to do – email, phone, text. It will increase attendance if you send it out at least two weeks in advance of the date, preferably a month (but not so long in advance to allow them time to forget it). A reminder a couple of days before the event by email or text is also a good idea.

Catering

Do you want to provide catering for guests and if so, what sort and who will serve? Will you pay for caterers or can you get friends or family to volunteer? You can usually buy wine and soft drinks on sale-or-return from local supermarkets, inclusive of glass hire. Along with a few crisps and nuts or canapés on trays, this may be all you need. Your book will stand or fall by its own merits. A bad book cannot be redeemed with expensive catering! Ask others to manage the catering at the event so that you do not get stuck handing round canapés when you should be signing books. Of course, the subject matter of your book may lend itself to themed catering, to create atmosphere and provide a bit of fun. A book about the history of Cornwall would definitely call for pasties, whereas a romance set in the Caribbean could be washed down with tropical fruit platters and rum cocktails!

Agenda

Schedule a specific start time for arrivals on the invitation. Decide whether you want to have a formal speech once they've arrived, perhaps an introduction by your publisher/the bookstore manager/museum curator, with a few words from yourself, or whether you prefer an informal atmosphere with no set piece.

Displays

Arrange your launch area neatly and boldly. If you have posters, pin them up on boards to show them off to best advantage. If you have postcards and bookmarks, fan them out on tables around the room, rather than leaving them in a pile. Create a talking point with relevant materials – perhaps originals of the illustrations used in your book, your source of inspiration or props to set the scene and create a relevant atmosphere. You might also want to play some background music, though not so loudly that it will kill conversation. Depending on the venue, you might be able to get away with an iPod and speaker to keep the costs down. If you are in a large public venue, check that it has a licence to play music.

Book Sales

Delegate the act of selling to someone other than yourself so that you can spend the whole of the event chatting with your guests and signing their books. If your event is not in a retail venue, make sure you bring an adequate cash float in a secure tin or box, the facility to issue receipts for anyone that needs one and if possible the means to take payment electronically. If you accept payment by cheque, ensure cheques are made out to the right payee and are properly completed. Take a note of the cheque guarantee card number on the reverse, particularly if you are dealing with someone you don't know, to ensure the bank honours the cheque.

Book Signing

Make sure you have plenty of pens of the right variety to write effectively on whatever paper your book is printed on. Have a comfortable table and chair set up for you, the author. Be wary of having a chair also for the book buyer, as this may encourage him or her to stay longer than you'd like! Be courteous and friendly to each person for whom you are signing, but try to keep the customers moving along – take too long over individuals and others may not be prepared to wait. If you are asked to write specific dedications, check how to spell the requested name. Have a pad of paper to hand for the requestor to write the name out. Better to ask for confirmation than to spoil a book with the wrong spelling. Have a glass of water to hand (or other refreshment of your choice) to keep you going. If you are nervous, you may get a dry mouth and need a drink to keep you oiled. (Watch any guest on a TV panel game and notice how much they always drink, even if they are used to public speaking.)

Photographs

Take some souvenir photographs of the event for promotional purposes. Don't worry about buying in the services of a professional photographer. You'll almost certainly have amongst your circle of friends a keen amateur with a sufficiently high quality digital camera to take a few pictures for your purposes. If not, seek out a photography student at your local college who will be happy to oblige in return for a reference and a link on your website. Your purposes are:

- To illustrate a news story about your launch event on your website.

- To provide a photo for any local news reports about your launch.

- To illustrate any future stories about you and your book – interviews in magazines, on book review blogs, etc.

Plan in advance what your volunteer photographer should snap: ideally a picture of you, head and shoulders at least, holding up a copy of your book so that the cover is clear and identifiable. The picture should be taken in a neat, uncluttered setting with nothing distracting in the background – but if you can include a backdrop that is relevant to your book, so much the better. For example, a picture used to promote Cotswold author Paul Newnton's novel about rural life was taken in fields near the village where he was born. On the other hand, if you've persuaded your local bookshop to host your launch for free, it's courteous to ensure that there's a bit of branding in the background. (Think of all those sporting interviews you see on the television where the sponsors' logos are in evidence.) Newspaper editors may try to cut them out, but it's courteous to thank the manager by trying to include them. Whatever the setting, you should be smiling, relaxed and proud. If you don't look enthusiastic about your book, don't expect others to be.

On a technical note, the camera should be set to a high resolution setting. This means the file size of each photo will be at least 1MB. Such a photo will look very clear in printed media. You can and should edit the photo before putting it on your website to make it lower resolution, as this will make the webpage load faster – but if you take a low resolution photo at the time, there is no way of turning it into a higher resolution photo afterwards. Don't worry if this doesn't mean anything to you – show this paragraph to your designated photographer and they will help you out.

Incidentally, if you are asking the local press and any relevant special interest media to attend your book launch – and you should – don't assume they will send a photographer along. These days, newspapers, especially local press, run on very low budgets and staffing levels and they have few photographic resources. Even the national dailies don't retain staff photographers any more. A local weekly paper may have just one staff photographer to cover all their needs and be dependent entirely on volunteers sending their own pictures in. Flick through a local paper and you will see that the photos taken by their staff photographer have a code number on them, enabling you to order copies – an important income stream for the paper. Any pictures without that number will have been sent in by readers and PR people.

Give-Aways

If you ever read about launch parties in the glossy magazines for films, fashion, fragrances and many other products besides books, you may have the impression that you're under obligation to provide goody bags or other free gifts to your guests. This is only true for high-budget events such as the Oscars or designer fashion shows, keen to lure high profile celebrities whose presence will endorse their product or event. As a self-published author, you are in quite a different league. Do not be embarrassed to be charging for copies at your launch. You will in any case be providing extra value by signing each copy to their specification, whether they are buying copies for themselves or as gifts for others. (To sell a few extra, let them know that you are happy to sign inscriptions for gift copies, now or later, for Christmas and birthdays.) If you want to give something away, you can distribute free copies of your promotional bookmarks or postcards. Most people will be very happy to take some for their own use as bookmarks in their newly purchased, personally signed book – or to pass on to friends by way of recommendation.

Which brings us back to the important subject of...

Cost

Beware of letting costs run away with you. Set yourself a budget when you start planning your event and stick to it.

Don't consider the sales value of the event to be limited to the number of copies you sell on the night. The event will have raised the profile of your book and paved the way for future sales. The dividends will continue after it is over.

After all your hard work writing the book, you may feel you deserve a bit of a fling to celebrate and be happy to foot the bill and hang the cost. You could treat it just like a birthday party – a special occasion simply to celebrate the birth of your book. And as long as you can afford it, that's absolutely fine!

Post Mortem

After your event is over, take some time to think about what worked well and what might have been improved. You never know, you might want to do the whole thing again sometime, either for another book, or to continue the promotion of this book elsewhere. But in the meantime, make sure that you've exploited your book launch to full advantage by supporting it with appropriate media relations activity – and that's what we'll be discussing in the next chapter.

10

Hold the Front Page!

Getting Media Coverage

All publicity is good, except an obituary notice.
Brendan Behan, dramatist

Your book launch may be the first time you employ media relations to boost your book sales, but it needn't be the last. If you're smart about how you use the media, you may even reach the point where the media starts to contact you for news, rather than the other way round.

Plenty of specialist PR agencies and consultants would be happy to take your money in return for a tailor-made media relations campaign for you. For the average self-funding author, this would be a prohibitively costly investment unlikely to be cost-justified by extra sales.

The good news is that you don't need a third party to attract press coverage. With strategic thinking, common sense and commitment, you should be able to achieve worthwhile results for next to no cost. This chapter will be a crash course in how to manage your own media relations campaign to promote the sales of your book.

If you are new to media relations, you may well find it a terrifying prospect. Recent scandals in the British media have seriously damaged the public's trust of reporters, but do not be alarmed. You are in quite a different league to MPs and celebrities who live their lives in the public eye. You and your new book are a gift to local journalists!

Before we proceed, you need to accept one universal truth about media relations: whatever you do, nothing will gain you guaranteed editorial coverage. It doesn't matter who you know or what you do, the only way to guarantee column inches is to buy them in the form of advertising.

Buying an advert may give you the feeling of having done something constructive but such confidence would be misplaced. Only in very rare circumstances will it be a worthwhile investment – for example if you have written a book for a narrow niche market served by a very specialised but well-read journal.

Local or special interest publications are notorious for persuasive advertising sales teams who will offer you cut-price space because they've "been let down at the last minute" or "really want to have you in this month's issue" or "will only charge you print costs". Do not be persuaded. Such an advert will not lead to guaranteed sales for an affordable fixed price. Whatever the salesmen tell you, the simple truth is that no matter how carefully you choose the media for your advert, all that is guaranteed is that the advert will appear in print. The self-published authors I canvassed for this book were scathing of their advertising experience, rating it as the most dispensable of their past marketing activities. If this sounds harsh, just think – when was the last time you bought a book because you saw an advert for it, knowing nothing else about it? I don't think I ever have.

Instead, your media campaign should focus on seeking editorial coverage. Although there are no guarantees of achieving column centimetres this way either, one thing is certain – if you don't try, you won't achieve any results at all. And if you do try, with well-judged strategy and tactics, you will almost certainly gain some media attention.

Before we proceed to specific instructions, let's first step back a moment and consider why you should pursue editorial coverage. Here are three reasons:

- Media coverage will spread news of you and your book to a much wider group of people than you can reach in person.

- Column centimetres in a respected publication imply external endorsement (even if the article merely reproduces the press release you have written yourself!) and therefore make people more likely to buy your book.

- You can reproduce these articles as collateral on your website and in other marketing publicity to extend your credibility as an author.

Next, what sort of coverage should you aim for? You might be surprised to learn that it's not necessarily a book review. Yes, positive reviews are great sales boosters, as is serialisation as Book of the Week on BBC Radio 4 or the sale of film rights to Steven Spielberg. Sadly, very few authors are fortunate enough to gain any of these valuable platforms, not least for reasons of space, and self-published authors will be way down the list of contenders.

This is because the attitude of newspaper editors is similar to that of bookshop owners. They see mainstream publishers as filters, selecting for them books of a certain calibre. There is also the hard financial fact that the national press favour publishing houses that spend large amounts to promote their whole catalogue, not just the few books reviewed. There are so many good, new books published each year, throughout the year, that reviewers will have more than enough to fill their columns from the mainstream publishers' books. They will be offered many more free books than they could possibly read. Reviewers are therefore extremely unlikely to give time or space to a book submitted by an independent author working on just one book. No matter how great your book is, the harsh truth is that any free review copy you send to a national reviewer will almost certainly be discarded unread.

This doesn't mean that you will never have a book review published. However, it does mean that you need to take a different approach. Instead of sending off free review copies to books editors, seek attention instead in the news pages of publications that will be interested in you.

Which publications will be interested in you? There are two sectors of the press that really are worth you addressing:

- Media who are local to you (not only the printed press but also broadcast media).

- Specialist media aimed at the niche market served by your book.

Choose carefully which local and special interest media to target. Bear in mind that dealing with the media is very time-consuming. It's best not to cast your net too wide, but to concentrate first on those that are most relevant, and then radiate out from there as time permits. If and when you've built up a really good following within these local and special interest media groups, you will have more clout to command the attention of larger, general interest and national publications.

Understanding the Local Media

Before addressing your local media, put yourself in the shoes of their staff for a moment. The advent of the internet and the facility it brings to contact anyone, anywhere, at any time for little or no cost, has laid down a huge challenge to the traditional local media. Even the longest-standing local papers are finding it difficult to remain profitable or even solvent while ploughing their traditional furrow: reporting on news and events on their patch. Some of the most respected papers have responded by reducing their frequency, replacing several editions of a daily (morning, lunchtime, evening, late) with a single edition once a day, or even telescoping them into a weekly. Many have also shrunk in size to reduce their costs as traditional advertisers (estate agents, landlords, car showrooms, employers) deserted them for other media with more penetration and faster response times. Why would anyone with internet access buy a local paper to find the first news of flats to let, houses to buy, cars for sale or jobs to apply for, when there are online equivalents with more up-to-date information instantly available?

Another strategy to remain viable in the face of reduced advertising sales and circulation figures has been to reduce staff. Local hacks and photographers have always earned very little and worked long, anti-social hours, but have been happy to do so to gain the experience required to get them better jobs with national media. Now there are even fewer of both, working harder than ever, to cover the same volume of news. Most local papers will have only a couple of reporters to fill all their pages and just one staff photographer who is sent in all directions to get their main news photos.

This makes it much harder than it used to be to pin down a reporter for a discussion or to lure one out to a launch event. This may sound like unmitigated bad news, but it's also good news because it means that editors are now much more open to the submission of unsolicited, strong local news stories, emailed in with relevant digital photos – and this is where you come in. If you can devise and submit timely press releases, in an acceptable digital format, profiling yourself as a local resident with a success story, supported by a clear, well-composed photo of you and your book, you have a very strong chance of your news story appearing in print, virtually word for word. If they have time, the reporters might get back to you for more details or to ask any questions left unanswered by your press release – but they are unlikely to have time. Therefore, your press release should be as complete and comprehensive as possible. Don't play hard to get or be mysterious. Instead of being intrigued, they'll probably just be irritated and dismiss your approach altogether. And don't treat the reporters as if you have a right to coverage: you don't. You have to earn it.

The other point to be clear about is that you should target only the local media who cover the area you're interested in. Their readers buy those papers purely because they want to know what's happening in their hometown, village or county. The editors will have very strict definitions of "their" territory. If you don't know what this is, visit the paper's website or phone its office for this information. Don't ask to speak to the editor or news reporter – they will already be overburdened trying to get their news stories together and won't thank you for wasting their time. If the paper is big enough to have a dedicated receptionist answering the phone, pump her for information, including the email address to which you should send your news story, the best time to send it so as not to clash with deadlines and any other helpful advice you can persuade her to impart. If there is a newspaper office that's open to the public (which very often exists to sell copies of newspaper photos to the public), ask there.

If a paper has already decided that it will cover only North West Bristol, for example, then even the most alluring photo and story from South East Bristol will go straight in the bin. Even if their definitions of territory seem to defy common sense – for example, a county magazine refusing to cover items about villages on its border – you are unlikely to change the editor's mind and persevering will only risk alienating him.

Just about every part of the UK will have at least one local paper that will consider you to be in its catchment area, and probably more than one. If you're not a regular local paper reader, stop by at your nearest newsagent or supermarket and browse their shelves. Don't just look at newsprint. There's probably also a "county" magazine that covers your area, and maybe even a local arts or book interest journal. Pick them all up: they're all fair game for you and your book. A file copy will be a worthwhile investment for you, but if you'd rather borrow than buy them, head for your local library, which will usually stock copies.

Have a good look through each one to familiarise yourself with the kind of story it likes and how it presents its news. I was once advised by a local press photographer, who had better remain nameless, that his brief was to take pictures to suit what the editor defined their typical reader to be: a middle-aged policeman. By this he meant conservative with a small c, respectable, reasonably intelligent but not an intellectual, interested in a little moderate titillation but fundamentally law-abiding and averse to scandal. No offence to any policemen reading this book! Start to read your local paper regularly and you'll soon spot news stories about other local authors. Examine how the paper has handled their news – what kind of photos they've used, how much information they've included about the book. Even if the authors and the books profiled are completely different to yours, you'll see what has earned them column centimetres and pick up ideas of what you need to do to gain yours.

It's not only local papers that you should be targeting with your news stories. You will also almost certainly be in reach of at least one local radio station in the regional network of BBC Radio. If you don't already know which is yours, visit www.bbc.co.uk/radio for a complete list.

Radio stations have a similar dilemma to the local papers, only they have airtime instead of printed pages to fill with new material, week in, week out. They also serve clearly defined geographical areas. Present yourself as a local resident with a good news story about the launch of your book (or indeed any later activities) and you will have a good chance of being granted an interview. Your approach should be similar to your newspaper strategy: an emailed press release with the main points of your story. It may seem counter-intuitive to add a photo – this is radio, after all – but they may well be interested in seeing what you and your book look like, and it makes a psychological difference to be able to put a face to the name should they talk to you later. This introductory package should be enough to whet their appetite for an interview.

The response of the radio station will be different to that of the local paper, in that they are very unlikely just to regurgitate your press release. Although they do run news bulletins, these are usually localised versions of national headlines, so quite dissimilar to local newspaper news stories. The most likely treatment by the local radio station will be to offer you an interview, either live on air or pre-recorded. Welcome this with enthusiasm and trust, even if the thought of speaking on the radio turns you cold with fear. If it's offered, embrace it! Local radio stations thrive on jolly chats with local people presented in a positive light. There are few "shock jocks" in this country. Your interviewer will do his or her best to make you feel comfortable and relaxed and to talk with authority and interest about your book. You may be invited into the studio if you live close by, or you may be offered a "down-the-line" interview. This means the interviewer phones your landline on a special high-quality telephone line that will come across crystal clear on the radio. (Many interviews on the national radio stations are done remotely, but you'd never know because the technology enables such clear transmission.)

If you're offered your choice of live or pre-recorded, choose pre-recorded, unless you're an adrenalin junkie. It makes for a more relaxed experience and will enable any awkward moments to be edited out. If live is the only option, seize the opportunity anyway. Your interviewer is very experienced at putting nervous guests at ease and will be slick at covering any hiccups along the way. Don't worry if you feel afterwards that you were incoherent. Transcripts of broadcast interviews often read very ungrammatically but are still understood and enjoyed by listeners.

There are local television stations also, but it is better not to approach these unless and until you have already built up a substantial media following via other local media. They have very few opportunities for interviewing local authors and your time will be better spent on other promotional activities.

Having talked at length about local media, it's worth noting that these don't have to be just local to where you live. If you have valid connections with other parts of the country, such as being born and raised elsewhere, you could have what PR types irritatingly refer to as "two bites of the cherry". Local papers in both areas will be keen to claim you as their own. Cotswold-born author Paul Newnton, now living in East Anglia, not only gained press coverage in Gloucestershire and Norfolk, but was also invited for a radio interview by BBC Radio Gloucestershire via the BBC Norfolk studio. John Rigg, author of *An Ordinary Spectator: 50 Years of Watching Sport*, is targeting both his childhood home of Leeds, where he first became a sports fan, as well as his current home in Scotland. In both areas he will doubtless find many fellow spectators keen to share his experience.

If you go about it the right way you are almost certain to be able to secure a book launch story, with a photo, in at least one local publication in the area in which you were born, especially if you can include with your modern publicity shot a photo of yourself in your birthplace – your face circled in the primary school photo, for example. It's also worth targeting your old school, college or university. Almost all educational institutions have alumni organisations these days, even if only a page on Facebook or Friends Reunited and it's worth flying the flag here. If you discovered a book by someone you used to sit next to at infant school, wouldn't you be intrigued? You might even buy it out of pure curiosity even if it was the kind of book you wouldn't normally read.

Equally if in your day job you belong to a professional or trade body, it's worth investigating whether there are easy inroads to publicity there. If you're a teacher, and you've written a novel inspired by your classroom experience, *The Times Educational Supplement* may be interested in running a news story about you.

All of these aspects of your life may seem irrelevant to the subject matter of your book – but they might just give your news story the edge in being picked out from a pile by a reporter.

I remember being very surprised at a book talk in a public library when the successful author of chick-lit books, Sarah Duncan, spoke at great length about her previous career as an actress. Many years before, she'd played the girlfriend of Rodney in *Only Fools and Horses* (his wife Cassandra's predecessor). I wondered why on earth she was going on about her TV appearance so much, especially when it was so long ago. Only afterwards did I realise it was a smart way of making her stand out from the crowd. And another gem: she has a City and Guilds qualification in Bricklaying! She's also very good at promoting herself online – see www.sarahduncan.co.uk.

Special Interest Media

You may already be an avid reader of the special interest media press to the book that you have written, especially if it reflects your profession or favourite hobby. In this case, you don't need me to tell you how to track them down.

If not, Google various keywords that might find publications appropriate to your book – e.g. for a book aimed at amateur stamp collectors, you might input "stamps, philately, stamp collecting, journal, official, magazine, hobby, collector, amateur". Check out carefully any that come up as titles can be deceptive. Early on in my career, I worked for a magazine publishing house that specialised in communications and military technology, with titles such as *Telecommunications* (of which I was the news editor), the frighteningly titled *Journal of Electronic Defense* and *Microwave Journal*. The latter was entirely to do with communications via microwave technology, but we were regularly approached by well-meaning PR people offering us the latest ready-meal or domestic microwave oven to test. They must have been puzzled why their request caused whoever took their call to fall about laughing.

Most special interest magazines will include book review sections and in this case, it may be worth approaching them to offer a free review copy of your book. Do not waste your precious copies by sending in one unsolicited: you should first send in a press release about your book (I'll tell you how to do this in a moment), enclosing a pre-paid reply card (if sending in writing) or an email address (if emailing your news) to make it easy for them to accept. Only when they have confirmed their interest, should you despatch a copy.

Whether or not you choose to offer a free review copy, you should certainly send them appropriate press releases. Once you've identified which press you're going to target with your news, make a checklist of the best individuals at each paper to which they should be addressed. Phone or email their switchboard/enquiry desk to get the right name and job title, and physical or email address (beware that many papers will have their advertising and editorial offices in different places). Be as precise as you can to ensure your press release reaches the most receptive reporter.

And now you're ready at last to write your press release!

What is a Press Release Anyway?

A press release (also often called a news release) is the starting point for a news story, stating the plain facts on which the journalist can build his report for publication. In the following pages, I'll assume we're talking about a press release to announce the launch of your new book, but the same rules apply to any news stories you might want to disseminate long after your launch is over, such as announcements of imminent book signing dates or reaching a spectacular milestone in book sales.

Most importantly, and perhaps counter-intuitively, your press release should be dispassionate. It isn't an advert and therefore should be free of hype, emotion and wild claims. You can quote someone else making a subjective statement about your book, if it's true, relevant and helps illustrate the strength of your story. To a journalist, there is a world of difference in credibility in a press release that starts out claiming "The best children's book ever about bird watching has been written by me, Robin Sparrow" and a measured, factual release that includes towards the end an accredited quote, such as "Sparrow's bird watching book will be a useful guide for any primary school aged child," says Dr Wren, RSPB Education Officer. "We're going to give one as a free gift to all new junior members of the RSPB."

Bear in mind that reporters are likely to have landing on their desk (or these days more likely in their email inbox), *dozens* of press releases, all vying for space in the news pages. Yours needs to grab their attention, convince them of its newsworthiness and be easy for them to transfer onto their newspaper's page.

It should therefore begin with a succinct and informative title that tells the reporter the gist of the news story at a glance e.g. "Rotherham teacher draws on classroom experience for new children's book on bird watching". Resist the temptation to pen a punning or entertaining title that you think would make a witty newspaper headline: "Sparrow hatches birdie book". It's the reporter's job to catch the eye of the newspaper reader. Your job is to convince the reporter that it's worth reading your press release because it will feed him an easy, relevant news story. And reporters like to think up their own exclusive headline. They'll be very unlikely to copy yours, no matter how clever it is, for fear of the same one appearing in the rival press.

You need to flesh the story out with human interest and detail. So as well as choosing the right title, you need to choose the best news angle. What is the most remarkable aspect of your achievement? What details will make your story more appealing? Did you write it as the result of an interesting life experience? "Rotherham teacher's new book on birds inspired by rare golden eagle nest on classroom roof." Is yours a particularly unusual achievement? "Rotherham teacher overcomes fear of feathers by researching new book about birds." Sometimes it's difficult to see these angles yourself so, if you're struggling, ask an interested friend's opinion. Above all, try to focus on the story *behind* your book, rather than the simple fact that you've written it.

"Do come up with fresh angles for the media and don't expect "author writes book" to make the news," advises Sarah Duncan, bestselling author of romantic fiction.

With a boom in self-publishing, it's not enough to simply announce that you've written a book. A journalist is likely to say "You and 10,000 others this year!"

The order in which you present the facts is important. The most significant points should appear at the beginning, with background details towards the end. You don't set the scene before you reach the punch line – the punch line is to be delivered first. To the uninitiated, it may even feel like you're writing it backwards. A typical press release might include the following paragraphs:

- News angle to engage the reporter's interest.

- Name of the new book's author, title and publication date.

- What the book is about.

- Details of the author, spelling out the local links.

- How the author came to write the book.

- Endorsements of the book by credible reviewers, if you already have any (e.g. specialists in the field at the heart of the book).

- Technical details of the book – retail price, format, ISBN and stockists.

- A highlighted note at the end offering a free review copy to the reporter, with instructions of how to request one.

- Extensive contact details including author's website, email address, mobile number and landline. Don't play hard to get – if they need further information from you in time for an imminent deadline and can't get hold of you, they'll give up and move on to someone else!

- The publisher's website and contact details.

- Links to an online source of book cover images, review copies and online sales.

If sending it by email, make sure the subject line of your email contains a snappy and attention-grabbing description. Reporters received hundreds, sometimes thousands, of unsolicited emails every day and only have time to open those that promise a good story, so spell it out to them. Many reporters will have learnt to spot good material within a few seconds, so make sure your subject line and opening sentences are exciting, well-written and promise something useful to their readers.

It is wise to send the press release in the body of the email, as well as in an attachment. But beware of sending too many attachments or large files, in case they fall foul of spam filters or message size limitations put in place by larger newspaper groups. Send your press release in PDF format to make sure they can read it, and in a Word or text format so they can edit it. Make sure any images have meaningful file names that link them obviously with your story, in case they get separated from the press release.

These days, you'd think sending by email would be sufficient, but personal experience tells me that it's always worth posting a hard copy too. I've been surprised at how often emails have bounced back from local papers whose email boxes have been full. There's no excuse for it with modern technology, but it's an indication of local media's budgetary constraints – and of how many other people are out there competing for the column centimetres that you want for your news story!

How to Take Press Photographs

Any local paper – and plenty of other media too – will be more willing to publish your news story if you are also able to provide interesting and relevant photos. As mentioned earlier, don't expect them to send a photographer out to take one for you – they are in very short supply and will be fully occupied with hard news coverage.

The paper will have a preferred style of photo so take one specifically to match their needs. The best research you can do is to read through your target paper and emulate the style of photos recently used.

The photo doesn't need to be taken by a professional, but if you can afford it, at least one short professional photo session is worth having to provide you with a good stock of top quality shots. Expect this to cost upwards of £100 per hour. Not all photographers are the same – many specialise in certain areas. Google "PR photographer" or "press photographer" plus your location to find one that is skilled at people-shots and located close to where you live (they'll charge extra for mileage so proximity is important).

If money is tight, you might find a friendly freelance or student who'd be happy to take yours in exchange for a recommendation on your website and a link to his online portfolio. Alternatively ask a friend with a decent camera to oblige.

If your photo shoot is carefully planned, it doesn't matter

who is behind the camera; it should result in good shots of you looking pleased and proud of your new book. Make sure your book is prominently featured and that its title can be clearly read. The press like photos which are tightly cropped to make best use of the space on the page, so home in on not much more than your head and shoulders with the book in front of you. They will probably crop out any extraneous background and can be pretty ruthless about it.

From his successful Pixel PR Photography[6] agency in Gloucestershire, photo-journalist Clint Randall shares some pointers gleaned from his seventeen years as a press photographer, latterly with the *Western Daily Press*: "Use an uncluttered backdrop to avoid distraction – but don't go for a completely plain setting or it will look like a passport photo. It's even better if you can set up the photo in a place relevant to the book. If your book is an autobiography, a location featured in your tale would go down well.

"If your book refers to your past, also send in what's known in the trade as "pick-up" shots. These are old snaps of you from times gone by, with an indication of where you are in the photo – a circle round the face of you as a schoolboy, for example. If you only have old prints of these shots available, photograph them with a digital camera or scan them at high resolution before submitting as a jpeg."

Finally, include a clear image of the book's cover.

"If the paper wants to include a close-up of your book, make it easy for them – the press likes everything served up on a plate!" says Clint.

All your photos should be emailed as attachments. Don't send just your favourite photo – the picture editor will like to

---

[6] www.pixelprphotography.co.uk A very gifted and creative photographer, fabulous at putting nervous subjects at their ease.

have a choice. Ideally, include both landscape and portrait formats so that there'll be one to fit whatever slot is available.

"Bear in mind that papers are usually written and printed at different locations, often many miles apart," says Clint. "Picture editors are generally working late at night after the journalists have gone home and they won't be able to pick up the phone to check a detail if something's not clear. So include a comprehensive caption for every picture. The perfect caption includes the fives Ws: Who, What, Where, When and Why."

It's vital to send the photos as separate files, not embedded within the body copy of the press release. Only then can they be easily duplicated, edited and cropped by the picture editor.

Incidentally, if you have a very fancy camera that can take very high resolution photos, make sure you don't choose too high a resolution. Too big a file might get rejected by the paper's email server. Many newspaper offices have it in their IT policy to reject emails over a certain size, no matter what they are. The file size should be about 1Mb to ensure clear reproduction on the printed page. Photos on websites can be of much lower resolution, because computer screens themselves are very low resolution. More dots per inch simply won't show up. High resolution pictures take a long time to load, tempting the viewer to click away from your page – something to be avoided at all costs.

Gaining Media Reviews

As suggested in the previous chapter, guard against sending out review copies without first confirming that your targeted journalist really wants a copy of your book. Reviewers have limited time to read books and there's no point sending them one of yours if they're not able to fit it in. Instead, send them a polite introduction offering a free review copy, making it easy for them to return a yes or no answer. Only send a review copy to those who positively confirm an acceptance. The invitation to review can be in various forms – an email, a formal letter or perhaps a colourful postcard showing an image of your book. If an email, they can RSVP by email. If a formal letter, enclose a reply-paid postcard with their details on it, addressed to you, or a tear-off slip and a stamped, addressed envelope. Try to make the invitation as enticing and intriguing as you can – but also a truthful and accurate foretaste of your book. If you create inappropriate expectations, don't expect an entirely sympathetic or appreciative review.

Of course it's not just the media whose reviews can be useful to you. All reviews will be good ammunition for your future publicity material, whether from professional print journalists, friends and family or online bloggers and reviewers. Make sure you harvest all the reviews that you can and use them to full advantage.

11

How Long is a Piece of String?

What to Spend in Time and Money

If you have to ask the price, you can't afford it.
JP Morgan, financier, in response to a question about the price of
maintaining a yacht

When it comes to the budget for promoting your book, decide what you can afford and cost-justify – and stick to it. Work out how much each book has cost you to print and the comparative margins to be made selling via retailers, both online and on the high street, by post and in person. Not every book sold will yield the same return, because different retailers expect different margins. You will almost certainly find that even if you are doing all the running yourself and have zero promotional costs, you'll need to sell an awful lot of books to make a significant income. In short, don't give up the day job!

It's worth setting aside a substantial number of sprats to catch those elusive mackerel. There are certain items that you should always try to afford.

"Send as many copies as you can afford out to reviewers," advises Amelia Fairney, Publicity Director at Penguin Books (General). "Invest in a good website and get networking in the real world too." (Take her advice, but also be wary of sending out unsolicited review copies, as discussed in earlier chapters.)

Of course, it's not just about the number of copies you sell. If your book is stocked by libraries, you will benefit eventually from Public Lending Rights even for a single copy, if you're lucky enough to exceed the minimum number of required loans to merit a payment. You may be fortunate enough to have spin-off sales of book-related merchandise. However, be on your guard against the invisibles that can mount up and, if ignored, quickly far outweigh profits:

- Travel costs to visit bookstores which take only half-a-dozen copies on a sale-or-return basis will most likely wipe out any profits.

- The cost of booking a stall at your local arts festival may equate to more than the average discount expected by retailers unless you manage to sell a significant number of copies at the event.

- Postage costs for books of any substance can be alarming, so make sure you weigh your book in a jiffy bag, and work out the postage before you fix your delivery charge.

Make sure you're aware of the cost implications of your actions so that you can make an informed decision about which activities are most worthwhile. If you find that some aren't profitable, don't rule them out. Sometimes activities that seem financially unrewarding can yield other types of profit: good networking opportunities, valuable press coverage and enjoyment.

One way to contain your costs is to do absolutely everything yourself. Many self-published authors are entirely happy to do things such as man the stall at the local literature festival, tout the book around local bookshops and libraries and talk to school groups or WIs. Rudolph Bader, author of *The Prison of Perspective*, sold his first print run of 1,000 books entirely by touring Waterstones stores all over the southeast of England. His second print run is also selling well. He found that once he'd had a couple of successful events (selling up to sixty copies at a time – pretty good going for an unknown novelist!), the regional managers of Waterstones began to mention him during their monthly meetings and soon his reputation went before him. It became much easier for him to set up dates…and soon stores began to contact *him* to invite him to do an event in their store!

For many authors, this taste of celebrity will be all part of the fun. To the general public, if you can flourish a copy of a professionally published book with your name on the spine, you *are* a celebrity.

Writer Shaun Ivory sums this up eloquently:

> Writing is not easy, but compared to selling, it is the lesser of the two. You must accept this. Otherwise try something else…otherwise stay out of the marketplace. Strive for that one moment when you can justifiably reply to any official who asks what your occupation is by saying: "I'm a writer". There's no other feeling in the world like it. Watch the change in their eyes, the longing, the grudging respect. It makes up for all those lonely hours hunched over a stuck script and blurred vision. *Take that keyboard and run!*

If you are a very busy person with many demands on your time – work, family or indeed writing your next book – you may be tempted to delegate your marketing tasks to a third party. You might find a helpful friend who will do it for love or a professional who will do it for money. Think carefully before opting for either. In all of this, remember that no-one will be able to speak with as much passion and conviction about your book as you.

No matter how willing the friend and no matter how much they love your book, if they don't have the skills or knowledge to promote it, they could do more harm than good. They might waste review copies by sending them to the wrong people or worse, alienate those you need to win over by approaching them in an unprofessional way. No reviewer or retailer will respond positively to being stalked.

A third party professing expertise and experience may sound like a better solution, but they come at a price, usually charging by the hour. After all, they are there to earn a living, not to pursue a hobby. They are not doing what they do for fun or for love. However, they do have their uses – and their contacts! Many PR professionals have spent their career forging relationships with people the average self-published author couldn't hope to connect with, and that's partly what you're paying for when you pay a professional.

If you decide to employ someone, make sure you agree the ground rules and the charges in advance, and ask to be notified in writing before they commit to anything else that will result in further cost to you.

Also, you should be aware that paying a professional promoter does not guarantee results. All it guarantees is that they will spend the agreed time on the agreed activities. They may be able to approach book reviewers and booksellers on your behalf with a professional pitch but their fee does not ensure you will get a published positive review or be stocked by a retailer. They are simply raising awareness of your book before the appropriate people. They are specialists in leading horses to water but they certainly cannot make them drink – though they might make the water look more appetising.

Don't allow yourself to become downhearted with all this talk in terms of profit and loss. Even those lucky writers contracted to mainstream publishing houses are unlikely to be making a living wage from their work. And you didn't write your book solely for financial gain, did you?

Don't get too hung up on the accountancy side of things. Keep careful records so that at the year-end, you'll be able to offset your expenses against your sales to keep the tax office happy. And if you end up earning enough profit to necessitate paying extra income tax – well, that's a good problem to have!

12

Post-script

Don't Start from Here

Tourist: What's the quickest way to get to the motorway from here?
Yokel: If I were you, sir, I wouldn't start from here.

If you have already published your book and are satisfied that:

- Your book is as good as it could possibly be.

- It sits comfortably alongside similar books on the shelves of bookshops and libraries.

- The jacket design looks as professional and desirable as any books by your competitors.

- The inside pages are inviting and easy to read.

- There is not a single typo or grammatical error anywhere in its pages.

then feel free to skip this last chapter. However, if any of these points make you feel slightly uncomfortable, please do read on. These few pages will give you the opportunity to make sure your second edition or your next book will sell even better than your first.

If you have not yet published your first book, then congratulations on being so well-organised as to be thinking about marketing it before it's even in print! This chapter will help you avoid the pitfalls that await new authors and increase your future sales success.

The Final Hurdle

You have laboured long and hard over your manuscript to get to the point where you are ready to publish. After all those anti-social hours hunched over your manuscript, you will no doubt be starting to relax a little, sensing you're finally on the home strait. In your enthusiasm to see your book in its finished printed form, please don't rush at the last hurdle. After all the time and passion you have invested in your book, you owe it to yourself to finish the job properly. If you do, your patience will be rewarded by greater sales.

You may be sick of the sight of your manuscript by now, but it's very important to proofread it and sub-edit it time and time again. Many highly successful authors re-draft their manuscripts ten times or more before they are content with their final product. This is not just to fine-tune the plot or characterisation or to correct facts. An error-free final draft will give you a much greater chance of ending up with a book that you will forever read with pride.

Beware of the Typo

The content of your finished book must be scrupulously professional. A typo, mis-spelling or grammatical slip-up is the sure sign of an amateur production. Just one error early in your book may be enough to prevent a reviewer from taking you seriously or a potential bookshop proprietor from stocking your book. Few authors have such flawless spelling and grasp of grammar that their manuscript will not benefit from the eyes of a third party. Running it through your PC's spellchecker is definitely only a starting point. Never let it approve or correct words automatically, unless you want to give your editor a good laugh. Getting a friend with an English degree to proofread, or your mum who's a teacher to mark it is no substitute for experienced proofreading and copy-editing by a professional who is used to the industry's high standards.

It's true that you don't have to be a good speller or grammar expert to be a great writer. When Brough Girling, author of over thirty children's books, gives talks to schoolchildren for the Readathon[7] charity, he horrifies their teachers by pointing out that flawless spelling and grammar are not essential for great authors. He cites his own dodgy spelling and that of his close friend the late Roald Dahl – but you will not find a single mis-spelling in any of their books.

When was the last time you found a typo in a Penguin paperback? And wouldn't you be astonished if you did? While I've been writing this book, I've been keeping an eye open for typos in the books I've been reading, which have included dozens of volumes from mainstream publishing houses and about six that were self-published. No prizes for guessing in which sector I found the most errors. I leapt up from my chair last night when I finally found a typo in a bestseller by M C Beaton (author of the *Hamish Macbeth* and *Agatha Raisin* series). I rushed to the dictionary feeling I was striking a blow on behalf of the self-published, only to discover it was actually me that couldn't spell the word in question. Yet in one self-published book (by a now defunct firm that shall remain nameless) I found about a dozen errors in the first chapter. For the rest of the book, I was constantly on the lookout for more mistakes, rather than being absorbed by an otherwise great

[7] http://www.readathon.org

story; and I'm a tenacious reader. Others may not be so generous. With so many other claims on our time these days, the average reader may simply get fed up with seeing typos and put your book down after one chapter, never to pick it up again.

All Hail the Copy-editor

Even those writers who are experts in spelling and grammar benefit from professional copy-editing. Copy-editing is much more than correcting typos. It includes checking for sense, spotting repetition, eliminating non-sequiturs, changing unlikely names (e.g. twenty-first century teenagers called Gladys) and other gaffes that might distract or annoy the reader. A series of tiny, polishing changes like this can make the acceptable exceptional.

There is no bestseller on the market that has not been put through this process by its publisher. Browse through the Acknowledgements page of any book and you will usually find profuse thanks to the author's editor. If you find yourself balking at the thought of someone changing a word of your prose, you need to grow a thicker skin. Learn the art of self-criticism and copy-editing and you'll produce much better copy. That's why ex-journalists make such good writers: while working for their magazines or newspapers, they've spent many hours redrafting. From Charles Dickens and Mark Twain to Tom Wolfe and Bob Woodward, good hacks write great prose.

You can find out more about good editing and how to hire a decent professional at the Society for Editors and Proofreaders (www.sfep.co.uk).

The Right Title

But enough of the inside of the book. We'll assume it's flawless. Other traps await you. First of all, there's your choice of title. Many books start off with a working title and change several times before reaching the publisher. Every book needs a title that is original, pronounceable, recognisable and meaningful. It should not include an uncommon word that no-one will be able to spell or pronounce, no matter how important that word is to your story. It's especially important now that so many people buy books online. If they can't spell your book's title, no search engine will find it for them. So if your publisher suggests you change your title, do it.

The Perfect Cover

So – great content, great title. Now you must make sure your book is well packaged. No matter how brilliant your copy, if its cover is not attractive, you're going to have a harder time selling it. This may sound shallow, but your cover will make the first impression, so it's got to be good. The commercial buyer sees thousands of book jackets in his career. He is well tuned to tell at a glance whether or not a book will look good on his shelves and whether his customers will want to pick it up and read it. Look around the shelves of your local bookshop: great jacket designs and snappy titles will jump out at you. Yours should be every bit as good as your competition.

The cover must be an effective summary, a persuasive advertisement for the content and a good indicator of the genre. Without blindly imitating other books in its field, your book needs at least to look at home among them. Readers look for books that resemble those they have enjoyed. If you have written a light-hearted Georgian romance, you need to target buyers of Georgette Heyer and the like. Take a look at the latest editions of her books to identify the current market trend. Be sure it is the latest edition: even bestsellers have regular re-designs to keep them in step with current fashions, so take no notice of the cover of a 1950s edition you picked up at the Oxfam bookshop.

It may sound so obvious as not to need stating, but the cover shouldn't give away the plot. (I am still fuming years after reading a detective novel whose illustrator had thoughtlessly posted the unlikely murder weapon on the cover, thus giving away the ending.) Think of it as a film trailer: it should be enough to lure you in, to make you want to buy a copy and to start turning those pages.

If you can get one, an endorsement on the cover from a well-known, successful author or other authority within your genre will help you sell more copies. Your target reader may not have heard of you, but if they like and respect your endorser, some of that loyalty will be transferred to you.

Your cover should also be a helpful indicator of the content and tone of the book; a shorthand, at-a-glance summary that will enable the casual browser to decide whether it's worth picking up and browsing.

This doesn't just apply to the front of the book. Your book will usually be displayed with only its spine showing, which means that the choice of typeface, font size, colour and so forth will also need to be eye-catching and smart. Some books even include a tiny illustration on their spine for added interest.

Finally, the typeface inside should match the tone of the book and the age and mood of the target reader. People take degrees in typography for a reason: they're learning how to make content readable and easily digested. Do your research and choose the right fonts. Restrict sans-serifs to headings and select a neutral, easy-to-read serif for the main body of your text. Study how the mainstream do it and work out how their line-spacing and type-size affects readability. Even better, hire a professional as they know what they're doing and will probably get it right first time, saving you hours of frustrated trial and error.

Play Mystery Shopper

If you're not convinced, next time you pass a second-hand bookstall or charity shop, spend ten minutes browsing the shelves and see what you think. Some books will look so much more appealing than others from their spines and their covers.

As an avid charity bookshop shopper, I often find a few books jump off the shelves. I've easily tracked down many series of books because their spine bears distinctive branding – those of Alexander McCall Smith are a great example, with really evocative African-themed typography and graphics. I can picture their covers and spines vividly in my head. By contrast, others stand out for their awfulness. In my old-fashioned head, I term these the "John Bull Printing Outfit Brigade", as they remind me of the home-made books we made as children using tiny toy moveable rubber type sets with ink pads.

Those books conspicuous for their unprofessional design are never the product of mainstream publishing houses, but are the work of a writer who has done his own design and paid his local printer to print them on his behalf. This is typical of titles produced by tiny religious cults, publishing their beliefs on a shoe-string via a local printer, clearly trusting that divine providence will make people pick them up. It doesn't.

Printer versus Publisher

A printer is not the same thing as a publisher. Printing is just one of the many tasks involved in publishing a book. A printer will simply follow the customer's instructions and produce a book from the manuscript given. He or she won't check for typos or advise on artistic impression. He'll just treat it like a commercial print job, in the same way that he might run off a batch of wedding invitations without commenting on the venue or choice of partner.

"Ah," you might say. "But I've got my own ISBN number

organised – doesn't that mean it's a proper publishing job?"
Sadly, it's not that simple. Technically, it will count as a published
book, but it won't give it automatic customer appeal.

Engage an Expert

There are very few writers, and even fewer new writers, who
can publish their own book to the very high standards
required of the modern commercial marketplace without
outside help. In the absence of a mainstream publisher, a
publishing consultant or reputable publishing service will be
an invaluable ally. Do not be put off by those who refer to
these companies disparagingly as "vanity publishers": these
days there are professional, experienced advisors out there
who will help make your book a commercial success. Engaging
the right publishing consultant will be a very worthwhile
investment that you will never regret.

Choose Your Partner

Partnership is the key word here: your relationship should
be of mutual respect and assistance. There are many
publishing houses that will be happy to help you (and take
your money) but not all offer the same service or value.
Don't be in a rush to choose one and don't base your decision
solely on price.

So what makes a good publishing partner?

- A designated personal consultant who will take the time
  and trouble to get to know you, your work, your target
  market and your ambitions.

- The provision of graphic design services by designers
  experienced in book layout (very different from designers
  of packaging or posters or advertising).

- An optional copy-editing and proofreading service by way of quality control.

- A proven track record in helping other authors similar to yourself to publish professional-looking, commercially viable books.

- The confidence to put you in direct contact with their satisfied customers.

- A clear, open and itemised list of charges and contractual obligations.

- Free initial contact and provision of an estimate (any company that charges you just to investigate their services is unlikely to be effective in its core business).

And here are some to avoid:

- Design companies who do not specialise in book publishing. No matter how impressive their portfolio of brochures or advertisements, they will not be aware of the subtle requirements of the book marketplace.

- Large agencies that are used to working on a grand commercial scale. I speak from first-hand experience, having worked for many years for large public relations and advertising agencies. These will not countenance any deal worth less than tens of thousands of pounds. In the current economic climate, some struggling agencies may offer to take on all kinds of contracts that they would not normally handle. Even if you do manage to negotiate an apparently reasonable deal with them, you will find yourself, as their smallest client, at the bottom of their list of priorities.

- Conglomerates who boast that they publish thousands of books every year. How personal is their service likely to be?

- Companies who wish to tie you in to a period of time. Check their contract and make sure there's a reasonable termination clause and that you retain the copyright to your own work. Believe it or not, there are some outfits that will prevent you from taking your own work elsewhere for a period of years.

Choose instead a company that describes itself as a publishing consultant or publishing services company (good key phrases to Google) and has a clear track record of providing the service you need to other authors like you. It may be small, it is unlikely to be a household name, but it will provide what you require and be a true partner in your success as an author.

Clearly I have a certain bias as my book is brought to you by the publishing consultancy SilverWood Books of Bristol (www.silverwoodbooks.co.uk), who commissioned this book as a helpful source of advice to its clients (which in itself speaks volumes about their standard of customer care). They have been enormously helpful and supportive, endlessly patient and unstintingly professional and I have no hesitation in recommending them.

But as the BBC likes to say, other publishing consultants are available. Whoever you choose, I wish you well. Anyone who has the imagination, determination, and energy to write a book deserves all the success they can find.

Please let me know how you get on and how this book has helped you. I'll be delighted to hear from you. Oh, and I'd love to read your book!

13

Conclusion: Keep the Plate Spinning

Maintaining Momentum

One way to keep momentum going is to have constantly greater goals.
Michael Korda, novelist

So, you've made your plan, done everything on your list to promote your book to your target audience, done it within your budget and your time-frame and you still have books left to sell. What next?

It's easy to let things grind to a halt, but don't down tools. A book rarely has a sell-by date unless it's building up to a particular event such as the next Olympic Games.

There are plenty of books that are now classics that only really came in to their own long after they were first published. A good book does not stop being a good book just because it was published a year ago or a decade ago or even last century.

So do not despair! Have a break, by all means, to clear your head and restore your energies (and to save up some promotional budget if need be). But do not give up and leave that pile of books to turn to dust in your spare bedroom. Consider the publication date as the first of many news hooks to capture public interest. Keep looking and you will find many more opportunities to keep talking about your book.

The only way you can fail is to stop trying.

Acknowledgements

Many thanks to everyone who has helped me in the research and writing of this book; not least my husband and daughter for their patience and understanding when I've said to them, "Not now! I'm writing my book!"

I've been inspired and motivated by the many self-published authors whom I've encountered via SilverWood Books (www.silverwoodbooks.co.uk), via my own consultancy Off The Shelf Book Promotions (www.otsbp.com), via social media and other more old-fashioned means. I've had the pleasure and the privilege of meeting, either in real life or across the ether, a very wide range of authors and illustrators, all passionate about their work. Many of these kindly shared with me their own experience of promoting their books and I really appreciated their feedback from the front-line.

Between them, these authors embrace many different genres (including some way beyond my normal reading comfort zone), but they all share a passion for their chosen topic. I've been inspired by their dedication, hard work and sheer determination to succeed. Even if their subjects don't appear relevant to your book, you may still benefit from their advice recorded in the following section, "Writers Talk". To find out more about any of them, please don't hesitate to track them down via their websites – I'm sure they would be very happy to hear from you.

It wasn't only self-published writers who provided helpful advice. Sarah Duncan, an established author of bestselling romantic novels, including *Kissing Mr Wrong* (shortlisted for the Romantic Novelists' Association's Novel of the Year 2011), was unwittingly helpful to me when I attended a public talk she gave at my local library, before I'd even thought about writing

Sell Your Books! My reason for attending her talk was that I'd just enjoyed one of her books, picked up in the library by chance, and I was curious to see what she was like. It was fascinating to see a master promoter at work and I immediately devoured every other book she'd written. (Oh, the power of the public library talk!) Much later, once I'd started writing this book, I approached her for some specific advice for the self-published and she helpfully provided her views and then published them on her blog: http://sarahduncansblog.blogspot.co.uk/2011/06/12-dos-and-donts-for-authors-promoting.html. A writing teacher as well as an author, she writes a mean blog that is worth reading, whatever kind of writer you are.

Hereward Corbett of the Yellow-Lighted Bookshop, based in Tetbury and Nailsworth, (www.yellow-lightedbookshop.co.uk) kindly shared his extensive insider knowledge of the retail book trade and gave me a much greater appreciation of how the bookshop proprietor views the self-published author. Every visit to either of his shops reminds me of just how good a high street bookshop can be, even in this digital age – if you're ever passing, do visit them and share the joy.

Amelia Fairney, Publicity Director at Penguin Books (General), was very generous with her time and expertise, responding at length to my endless questions and helping me understand the mainstream publisher's perspective on the modern marketplace for books. Her helpfulness also cemented my long-standing passion for all things to do with the Penguin brand – been there, got the mug, got the t-shirt!

Brough Girling is the founder of Readathon, the children's reading charity that's helping raise future generations of eager recreational readers to the benefit of all authors. He is also a children's author who has spent many years promoting books – both his own and those of others. I have learnt a great deal from Brough about the way people choose, buy and read books.

I'm very grateful to the first official reviewer of this book, Dr Alison Baverstock, a highly experienced publishing professional and writer who is currently Course Leader of the MA in Publishing at Kingston University. She also generously agreed to write the foreword. You can find out all about her at www.alisonbaverstock.com.

Finally I owe huge thanks to Helen Hart, director of SilverWood Books, for commissioning this book. Helen is a successful writer, a voracious reader and a highly professional publishing consultant who spreads her infectious enthusiasm for all things bookish. Having worked with her on this book, I can understand why she has an ever-growing reputation as a meticulous, expert and caring advisor who gives her clients the very best chance of creating beautiful books that sit comfortably on bookstore shelves alongside books from the big publishing houses. Thank you, Helen, and your excellent team, for pointing me in the right direction, filling in gaps in my knowledge and helping me keep one jump ahead of the ever-changing publishing market.

And last of all I thank you, the reader (and writer), for buying my book. However you have published *your* book, I wish you the very great success that you crave and deserve. Now get out there and – *Sell Your Books!*

Writers Talk

Rudolph Bader

Novelist
The Prison of Perspective ISBN 9781906236205
Publisher: SilverWood Books
www.rudolphbader.com

Rudolph Bader's debut novel is a memorable, carefully crafted story intertwining the lives of three very different characters. Careful planning was required to fit marketing activities into the holidays from his full-time job as a university professor in Switzerland. He staged not one, but three book launches – one in Eastbourne (his base when in Britain) and two in Switzerland. Then, over eighteen months and armed with 2,000 promotional bookmarks and postcards, he squeezed in twenty-six book signings all over the south of England – a schedule that even Stephen Fry would be proud of!

Rudolph also appeared at the London and Frankfurt Book Fairs and gave several talks to literature departments in universities, at literary conferences and in book clubs. Doubtless his standing as a professor of literature personally acquainted with famous authors of our day will have helped open some doors, but Rudolph does not depend on existing contacts to make his sales. When staging bookshop signings, he approaches strangers who have no idea who he is and uses his impeccable manners, tact, and charm to engage their interest. (The intriguing title and mysterious cover image of his book jacket must also be of help.)

Rudolph's boldness pays dividends: his first print run of 1,000 sold out and he has now sold over 1,500 copies. Not surprisingly, he rates those marketing activities which involve interpersonal contact as the most effective for him: "book signings, talks to special interest groups and interviews". If starting over, he would aim for "more interviews".

Despite his significant sales figures, Rudolph is driven by conviction rather than profit.

"My aim is artistic, not commercial," he says. "I have always wanted to write novels. I have read, written about and taught literature in several languages for over forty years, and I know many contemporary authors personally. When I re-read my manuscript after a certain time (with a certain distance and the professional eye of a literary critic) I found it had turned out quite well and it merited publication. After all, many novels of far inferior quality are being poured out even by large commercial publishers."

His advice to the novice author is shrewd and comforting: "When you write your novel with commercial success in mind, make sure you show all the best qualities of your novel in the first three chapters of your text. Agents and publishers will only read the first three chapters and make their decisions on that basis, often missing out on the finer qualities of your novel which need more space to unfold. They are not literary people, but short-sighted business people, and their decisions don't depend on literary quality but on personal taste. When you receive a rejection slip do not despair. It need not be a flaw in your text; it's more likely you caught the decision-maker in the wrong mood. So my most important piece of advice is: Don't give up, and above all continue to write."

Richard Denning

Author of young adult sci-fi and historical fiction
Tomorrow's Guardian ISBN 9780956483560
Yesterday's Treasures ISBN 9780956483584
The Amber Treasure ISBN 9780956810311

The Last Seal ISBN 9780956810335
Child of Loki ISBN 9780956810328
Publisher: Mercia Books
www.richarddenning.co.uk

Richard must be the most energetic and enthusiastic self-promoter and networker of any of the self-published authors I have ever met. So far he has sold over 400 copies of his books (in print and e-book format) and gives away free copies to review sites. He is a prolific blogger, writes guest posts on other people's relevant blogs and uses blog tours to spread the word further via online reviews. He keeps himself in the limelight on Facebook by posting daily status updates about historic events that happened on this day in previous years – always worth a read. He is developing an ever-wider circuit of school tours with an ingenious mix of themes, all relevant to his books. His young adult novels revolve around time-travel to key moments in history, and so he offers different school talks to address not only English classes but also Science (regarding the physics required to facilitate time-travel) and History (discussing the specific eras in his books).

"School trips are looking good," he admits. "I sell a guaranteed number to the library and to the children as well. You often have to mailshot twenty to get one reply, but as I do more school visits I hope word gets around." (Personally, I think a five per cent success rate for a mailshot is pretty damn good!)

Richard is generous in sharing his experience with fellow authors, including learning from his early mistakes: "I have not yet recovered my costs, partially due to *huge* mistakes I made in the early stages, such as ordering large numbers before proofing them, buying hardback books, not paperbacks, etc. I also had had all the books edited and have covers made (all of which costs). But I am getting more income this year so

I would hope to recoup investment in time. I am monitoring costs and income carefully."

What does the wisdom of hindsight tell him?

"I don't think adverts had any benefits. Establish an online platform. Become active on social media from very early. Get blogging earlier. Forget adverts."

Here is his advice to newcomers to marketing a self-published book: "The road to self-publishing is long and hard work. I think many people hear the stories of "Amazon bestsellers for a day" or the self-published authors who have sold one million e-books and think it is easy. It is not easy. For most of us it is a grind. You have to decide: are you willing to commit to the long haul? I have only been doing it for about eighteen months and so only time will tell if I have the stamina and success. I can see that there is potential to succeed and am willing to push on with it."

Shaun Ivory

Thriller writer
The Judas Cup ISBN 9781906236212
No More Heroes e-pub ISBN 9781906236922
Publisher: SilverWood Books
www.shaun-ivory.com

Shaun's first thriller, *The Judas Cup*, sold out of its first print run and is now on its second. *No More Heroes* is currently available as an e-book for a range of devices including Kindle, and Shaun's currently at work on his third, *America Made Me*. Part of his success has come from targeting the most relevant market – Ireland. He manages his own website which also showcases his journalism. (He's sold numerous magazine articles in addition to his books.)

Here is this established author's advice to first-timers

(I've already quoted some of it earlier, but it's such good and heartfelt advice that I make no apology for repeating it here!):

> Once you've written your book, you have to have the courage of convictions, there's no real point otherwise. Go for entertaining and informative, everyone responds to that formula. The skill is in reaching the right balance. No matter how much time you spend on the book, with self-publishing, the onus is on you to sell it. Even with established publishers, unless you are a bestseller, you will still have to sell yourself and the product. In effect, they are one and the same. You must get this fixed in your head and keep it there. You will forget but sales and falling interest will remind you. The easiest part is writing. Writing is not easy but compared to selling it is the lesser of the two. You must accept this...otherwise stay out of the marketplace. Anyone within reason can write one book; manage another two or three and you are a writer, successful or not. Strive for that one moment when you can justifiably reply to any official who asks what your occupation is by saying: "I'm a writer". There's no other feeling in the world like it. Watch the change in their eyes, the longing, the grudging respect. It makes up for all those lonely hours hunched over a stuck script and blurred vision. *Take that keyboard and run!*

Paul Newnton

Novelist
The Witch at Happy End ISBN 9781870167444
More Witchery at Happy End ISBN 9781870167451
Tales from Barrow Magna ISBN 9781870167468
Publisher: Peter Francis Publishers
www.happyendbooks.wordpress.com

Paul Newnton's gentle tales of rural life are set in and around a fictitious Cotswold village for which it's been relatively easy to gain interest within the Cotswold district. Encouraged by sales of his first book in the series, fostered by good coverage in local papers, a local BBC Radio station interview and placement in his local independent bookshop ("as seen in this week's local paper/heard on local radio"), Paul has gone on to publish the next two volumes in his series and more sequels are in the pipeline.

His online presence makes it easy for readers who have enjoyed the first book to track down subsequent additions to the series. The books are also very easy to spot on the bookshop shelf as there is strong branding across the covers of all three books. Investing in this consistent and themed approach is paying dividends as his sales figures continue to rise.

Jill Rutherford

Author of travel memoir
Cherry Blossoms, Sushi and Takarazuka: Seven Years in Japan
ISBN 9780956967909
Publisher: Little Wren Press
www.jillrutherford.wordpress.com

As its title suggests, Jill's book is a memoir of a long spell living and working in Japan. She went there knowing no-one, speaking no Japanese and with no formal qualifications as an English language teacher. Even so, through determination and sheer hard work, she managed to set up her own successful language school, allowing her to spend seven years getting to know better the country with which she had fallen in love. Jill loves writing and is now working on her second book.

A good lesson learned from Jill is to maximise local publicity opportunities wherever you live, even though that location may have no immediate bearing on the subject of your book. In Jill's case, this is now Eastbourne, and not Japan. She held a meticulously organised launch party at the local Town Hall attended by the Mayor. She also worked with her nearest branch of Waterstones to set up an in-store book signing and she's involved with the local writers' group and arts festivals. Alongside these activities, she rates her website as one of her most successful promotional tools.

Pip Westgate

Author of children's novel
Bear and the Gitxsan Child ISBN 9780956225009
Publisher: Pip Westgate Books
www.pipwestgate.wordpress.com

Pip Westgate's first published novel is a gripping adventure in an unusual setting – the wilderness of Western Canada. It combines problems children face in the real world – parents' marital break-up – with the traditional myths of native Canadians (the Gitxsan tribe of the title). For Pip, selling enough copies to cover costs is only part of story, and his philosophical approach demonstrates the pride and satisfaction to be had even when your expectations of sales are modest. Profit really is not the only measure of a book's success.

> I felt I had some good ideas and a good story or two in me and so it seemed a waste not to record these. The idea of creating and sharing my own stories was the most attractive thing. I certainly never really expected to make a great deal of money from it. It was more the idea of taking pride in knowing it was something I had created and knowing that others had enjoyed it. I enjoyed the actual process of creative writing very much. I once

used the simile that writing the book but not publishing it was like preparing a *cordon bleu* meal but only eating it by yourself. Having produced something that I was pleased with (not that I'm suggesting my book is exactly *cordon bleu* equivalent!) it seemed a waste not to have it out there for others to enjoy. Knowing that other people have read and enjoyed your book generates a great deal of satisfaction and pride.

Pip continues, "The cost for your first couple of hundred books these days, with digital printing, is not prohibitive, and even if it doesn't lead to fame and fortune, it's still a cool experience to hold your own book in your hand and share it with others."

Pip's advice to those starting out in marketing their self-published book: "Build up a clear strategy for marketing prior to getting the book published. Approach libraries to book author talks and events – the same with schools. Put a lot of work into exactly what these will involve: you can't just say 'Look, I wrote a book'!"

Notes

1   Best Sellers, *The Times*, Saturday 1 January 2011

2   Source: Wikipedia http://en.wikipedia.org/wiki/Books_published_per_country_per_year

3   Source: The National Literacy Trust http://www.literacytrust.org.uk/reading_connects/resources/331_the_literacy_hour_in_primary_schools

4   http://www.bookstart.org.uk/about-us/about-booktrust/

5   http://www.readathon.org

6   www.pixelprphotography.co.uk A very gifted and creative photographer, fabulous at putting nervous subjects at their ease.

7   http://www.readathon.org

Printed in Great Britain
by Amazon.co.uk, Ltd.,
Marston Gate.